ROUNDS TO OURS

setting the mood and cooking the food:
menus for every gathering

photography by kristin perers

Publishing Director: Sarah Lavelle
Creative Director and Designer: Helen Lewis
Editor: Imogen Fortes
Photographer: Kristin Perers
Food Stylist: Aya Nishimura
Recipe Testing and Development: Kat Mead
Prop Stylist: Tabitha Hawkins
Additional Styling: Rosie Birkett and Linda Berlin
Production: Emily Noto and Vincent Smith

First published in 2017 by Quadrille Publishing,
Pentagon House, 52–54 Southwark Street,
London SE1 1UN
www.quadrille.co.uk

Quadrille is an imprint of Hardie Grant
www.hardiegrant.com.au

Cataloguing in Publication Data: a catalogue record
for this book is available from the British Library.

ISBN: 978 184949 959 0

Note: All oven temperatures refer to conventional
ovens. For fan ovens reduce the temperature by
20 degrees.

INTROD

Like all the best and most famous partnerships, we met at a jumble sale while wearing bumbags. From our first words to each other, commenting on a vat of chilli that was being sold by the paper cup, it was clear that our common ground was food: buying it, cooking it, eating it. We were both struggling to forge our careers in similar industries – TV and radio – so we had a lot of time and not much money. We'd either cook for each other every week, or try a place for a cheap lunch that we couldn't otherwise afford for dinner (daytime set menus are the frugal restaurant-lover's secret weapon, it turns out).

Hosting was our mutual passion – getting everyone around a big table, laying out a feast and creating that warm feeling that comes from full stomachs and noisy chat. The beauty of having people round for a meal is the bustle and commotion of an evening shared, coupled with the intimate feeling of being a guest in someone's home. A few months after we met, we decided to set ourselves a challenge: could we make our lunch 'club' bigger and open the doors to our homes to cook for other people? Not just friends, but complete strangers?

When we started our supper club we didn't *exactly* know what a supper club was. So we made up the rules. To the first one, we invited as many people as we had chairs (16); we decorated the table with hyacinth bulbs and served slow-cooked lamb and lemon posset. We accidentally grilled the lamb and the room was so warm that the flowers wilted before the dessert came out. But people stayed until the wee small hours and staggered home with new friends' numbers in their phones. We marked that one up as a success.

UCTION

Fours years on and we have learned a lot. As home cooks we know the pitfalls of throwing a dinner party (we once had to make 12 lemon tarts before we got a single one that was successful), but having run the supper club we also know great cheats, shortcuts and tips that make hosting that bit more breezy. Here they are in one place.

This is a book of menus: 24 occasions when we have welcomed people round to ours, and we hope to make you feel like you might want to do the same. It will help you decide what to cook, but also how to set the mood and make the most of your space. It will, we hope, take the stress out of entertaining.

I'm sure, like us, you have a shelf of recipe books that you rely on. If we want the ultimate chocolate fudge cake, we dig out a Nigella. If we need a great vegetarian curry, we turn to Anna Jones. But if we are racking our brains for a full spread for six friends on a Friday night, we sometimes struggle to find one source. So we thought we'd write just that book.

The food is really important but don't forget, having people round is about sharing a great night. It's hard to go wrong with fun people, lots of booze and a killer playlist – even if you do serve pineapple and cheese on sticks.

Use *Round to Ours* as a guide – for inspiration, ideas and insights. It's not meant to be dwelled upon too much, if we're honest – it's only dinner, after all. There's no point in crying over spilt milk, never mind burnt lemon tarts.

the
mood

music

———

We don't just stick on music for when guests walk through the door – setting the mood is as important for the person doing the cooking as it is for the people coming to eat. So while we are doing our prep we like to listen to something relaxing. French radio station Fip is a trusty choice; anchored by women with soft dulcet tones, they usually play music we have never heard before – everything from rap to jazz. We have absolutely no idea what's going on though – we have one GCSE in French between us! But being oblivious to the chat of the DJs actually helps us to focus.

On the night, music plays a really big role and no supper club would be complete without the record player. We delve into Jon's (Laura's boyfriend) extensive Northern Soul record collection and guests are encouraged to put on records and bring their favourite vinyl.

Make sure the volume is low enough for conversation to flow but loud enough to create atmosphere.

Our top 10 soul records:

Two Can Have a Party | Marvin Gaye and Tammi Terrell
Getting Mighty Crowded | Betty Everett
Soul Time | Shirley Ellis
He Was Really Sayin' Somethin' | The Velvelettes
You're Gonna Need Me | Ted Ford
Night Train | James Brown
Green Onions | Booker T. and The M.G.s
Tainted Love | Gloria Jones
You Hit Me Like TNT | Linda Jones
Take Me In Your Arms | Kim Weston

If in doubt, or lacking a turntable, make a playlist on Spotify, or enlist your most dedicated muso friend.

There are, of course, those times when you just need something last-minute – a guaranteed crowd-pleaser – and a film soundtrack is perfect for such moments.

Our favourite film soundtracks for a dinner party:

Amélie
Drive
The Virgin Suicides
Trainspotting
The Graduate
Pulp Fiction
The Descendant
Help!
Purple Rain
Dirty Dancing
The Breakfast Club

lighting

We have been in many dinner situations where we've found ourselves sitting under a million spotlights or one central bulb. When you are trying to create atmosphere or mood, turn off or turn down all ceiling lighting and illuminate the space with lamps. Strings of festoon lights that interconnect are great to light an outdoor space and can be brought out for any event – we bought ours online and we have used them at every gathering since.

Candles are a really inexpensive way of setting the tone: the rolled beeswax variety creates a warm light and can double up as a table ornament in beautiful candlesticks. We always have a scented candle burning in the room – earthy fragrances like amber and sage in winter and lighter floral notes like orange blossom or geranium in summer. It's worth investing in a good-quality scented candle: our go-to brand is Diptyque as they last for ages. We also love Haeckels and Earl of East. You only need to burn a candle for a few minutes for the room to be smelling wonderful all evening.

plates, platters and cutlery

——

For as long as we have been running the supper club we have used Falcon enamelware. We would love to tell you it was the plates' utilitarian look and beautiful striped edges that fitted in with our grand style master-plan, but in all honesty they are just the most practical piece of kit we use: stackable, lightweight, unbreakable and practically non-stick. Plus, in a small apartment they are handy space-savers.

We intersperse these with our ceramics: we often find lone pieces at car-boot sales rather than sets, so none of it 'goes together' but this adds character. If you want to be adventurous then why not sign up to a ceramics class and make your own? Granted this may be a lengthy process (everyone can use paper plates until you've finished the set!), but the results are so rewarding.

Large platters are very practical for big lunches or dinners; guests can just help themselves rather than you having to fuss with individually plating food. There are some really fabulous ones in the likes of The Conran Shop or Liberty London but they don't have to be expensive – platters are usually the items that go into the sale. We bought most of our serving platters second-hand and they were really inexpensive (change from a fiver!). It's worth having a selection of different styles for different occasions: plain, patterned, ceramic, contemporary and wooden, for everything from canapés to pasta. At our Scandinavian supper club we went for the D.I.Y. option and served the starters on wooden boards that we salvaged from a local skip. We cut them to size, sanded and cleaned them up – quite a job, but it was worth going the extra mile, especially as they were free!

Cutlery for us should be clean and simple and it's worth investing in a set – vintage or new. We have a great set of timeless ivory-handled cutlery that we picked up from a seaside town (it's always worth a detour via the charity shops).

glassware

—

Formal stemmed wine glasses can feel quite traditional.
We have no rules when it comes to what we serve our drinks
in – cocktails in our favourite amber tumblers from Duralex;
fizz in our shallow stackable glasses; and coffee in recycled
glass yoghurt pots bought in French supermarkets. Don't
be afraid to have a mismatched selection on your table. And
for table water we save handsome old bottles and refill them.
Try adding a little cucumber, coriander, mint or grapefruit
– this also brings a subtle hint of colour to the table.

linens

We have this nosy habit, wherever we go, of finding out where the linens are from, whether it's the crisp bedsheets in a hotel or the napkins in a restaurant. Don't feel cheeky about asking, most people love to share information. Once, on a trip to Mexico we traced the origin of the napkins to a man in an Oaxaca forest, then had them shipped back to the UK – we know this sounds pretty extreme for napkins but it just goes to show anything is possible (and the lengths we will go to for a bargain!). They are now one of our most treasured and most used possessions.

For our first few supper clubs we used IKEA tea towels as napkins. They are cheaper than a bag of crisps and they can look really chic (honestly). We cut the labels off and starched the hell out of them, folded them artfully and hey presto! We still bring them out for dinner parties now and we are always asked where they're from.

In charity shops, antique fairs and car-boot sales, tablecloths with imperfections, marks or holes will often be marked down in price, but if you are layering several then you can cover them up. You can mix different fabrics and textures to cover a large table. Going to the haberdashery and getting offcuts of fabric can be useful for table runners and if you're nifty with a sewing machine or, like us, you love Wonderweb, then you can finish the edges yourself.

finishing touches

———

When it comes to serving up, it's best (and easiest) to keep
things as relaxed as possible; informal and plentiful is
far more inviting than rigid and sparse. Then, by adding
a few flourishes, a simple sharing plate can be brought
to life. If you don't have enough ramekins, for instance,
why not use big sharing bowls for mousse or Eton Mess?

Think about textures and colours, even when it comes
to your food. In winter, try brightening up a piece of slow-
cooked meat by finishing with some apricots or pistachios.
In summer, salads really benefit from a scattering of pea
shoots or torn herbs, and a big dollop of aïoli will bring
humble beans to life.

A mandoline is really useful for making quick and rough
salads with kohlrabi, radish and celeriac; it doesn't need
to be precise but will look great – we use ours all the time.

Edible flowers are a fantastic way of adding something
really special to any simple dish – sweet or savoury. There
are so many ways you can use them – crystallise them, make
floral sugars (lilac is a favourite) or dry them. Rose petals
look like jewels when scattered over chicken and a handful
of fresh scarlet nasturtiums in a bowl of green leaves looks
spectacular.

You can buy them online or at some greengrocers but
growing your own is a much cheaper option. We buy ours
already started from Herbal Haven (herbalhaven.com).

place settings

—

At the supper clubs we always have a table plan: people like direction and can feel lost if they don't have an allocated seat. It's also a way for us to be strategic and encourage guests to meet new people. We always want to steer away from anything too twee (we are not wedding planners) so we prefer to replace traditional name cards with something a little more unique. We often tie names to herb bundles or attach brown tags to personal table gifts.

Guests love to have something to take away with them, so we tend to make extra of one element of the menu – for example, for our first supper club we made a rosemary-infused oil (to rub on lamb) and we put the spare oil into brown apothecary bottles sourced from Wares of Knutsford. At another evening, when we served deep-fried courgette flowers, everyone's gift was some courgette seeds in a little brown envelope to plant at home (though one guest did eat them!).

We have a typewriter and at the start of our supper club adventure we used to buy really good paper from the stationer's or online from GF Smith, and type out the menu. We played around with textures and paper stocks – one of our favourites was a translucent peach paper.

flowers & plants

The past few years have seen a real resurgence of the use of flowers and plants in interior design. It wasn't that long ago that terrariums weren't available in the UK and 'indoor plants' used to mean a spider plant in the school art room. Flowers have become way more relaxed, unfussy and frivolous (no more stuffy centrepieces) and plants have become a dinner-party table staple.

Flowers, like fruit and vegetables, are seasonal, which will always help with keeping your table updated. Soft, pastel, dusty, full-headed blooms in summer are a good contrast to hearty foliage and climbing branches in winter. In summer, you can create a lovely-looking table simply with the addition of lavender plants, rosemary or mint, and they will also create a wonderful fragrance. In the colder months, mini squashes provide a wonderful burst of colour for the table.

Flowers and plants don't just have to sit on the table: we once hung giant allium flowers upside down from the ceiling of the flat. Try it with big bunches of foliage and herbs, too. We tend to steer away from displaying flowers in standard vases, preferring Kilner jars, glass tumblers, ceramic pots or bottles.

And it's really easy to add a flourish to the table by using smaller herbs and flowers, fresh, dried or pressed. For an autumnal supper club we pressed bright-red leaves and had these resting on the menus. We've done the same with meadow flowers then attached them with a gold paperclip. Taping fresh flowers to napkins using neon tape looked great too. A tie of seasonal herbs on each napkin looks lovely – this is something we have done when we have been short of time. Even a little sprig of rosemary would be enough to lift a really simple place setting.

greenery tips
– Visit flower markets for wholesale prices
– Try the garden centre for succulents and herb pots
– Press individual flowers from a bouquet you have received
– Dry out bunches of hydrangea heads or eucalyptus – the latter are particularly nice in the bathroom as the steam brings out the scent
– Get inspiration online: our favourite green Instagram follows are @wormlondon, @graceandthorn, @ruby_marylennox, @putnamflowers, @nicamille, @thejungalow, and @conservatory_archives.

shopping

Over the years we have built up an eclectic selection of glassware, plates and table knick-knacks from our travels and there is no time like the present to start hoarding. Here are some of our favourite stores for a virtual rummage-through.

Etsy – vintage and handmade wares from all over the world. Try searching for linen, lighting, vases and candleholders. Most people are happy to post if you can cover the postage (ask even if it says they don't post outside the US).

eBay – true bargains are still out there. Be specific and check back frequently (get the app).

Amazon – ideal for next-day essentials.

Gumtree – a surprising treasure trove for house plants. Find established growers for a fraction of the garden-centre price.

Duralex – very inexpensive glasses in many styles; try Bistro, Manhattan, Gigogne, Provence and Picardie Amber.

Fish Eddy's (US-based but they ship to the UK) – vintage restaurant surplus.

Labour and Wait – enamelware in fantastic shades and utilitarian kitchen accessories.

Kana London; Anna Jones Ceramics; Suite One – handmade ceramics.

The Cloth Shop; Stella Dallas – vintage linens of all shapes and shades.

on your travels

Whenever you go away, whether it be
a work trip, a weekend to the countryside
or two weeks' holiday on a beach, always
leave some empty space in your suitcase
and pack a towel to wrap up delicate
treasures. Before you leave home research
the local flea markets, second-hand stores
and charity shops – save them on your
phone map so they are easy to locate
when you are in situ.

The Internet is, of course, an essential
resource when finding these places, but
there is nothing like a good tip from a local.
Send out some emails or a shout-out
on social media and get as many word-of-
mouth pointers as you can. Follow the
perpetual travellers on Instagram and
search via hashtags for hidden gems.

Our best market tip requires you to be
a bit ballsy. No matter where you are in
the world, give haggling a go. Be confident
and ask, 'What's your best price?'. This
has worked for us many a time – with the
local butcher, at an Italian flea market
(just not in Topshop!).

the larder

store cupboard magic

———

'Cheat's ingredients' was the working title for this section, but that sounded like we should be feeling guilty when in fact we are proud of these hard-workers. These are the items that we reach for time and time again to pack in a punch of flavour. They are great time-savers, but most of all each and every one of them gives a new dimension to any dish they're added to. We like ingredients that can multitask – able to raise the game of a cheese sandwich, avocado on toast or a bowl of pasta.

These aren't for the weekly grocery list – they will last you a long time, and some are more serious investments. But they are nice things to give and receive as presents. So when your Great Aunt says to you, 'What do you want for Christmas?', suggest one of these (otherwise you're getting that sock selection again). We always scour markets and supermarkets when we're on holiday to pick up local condiments too; usually they are quite cheap and you will get something different from the same old choices at home. Alternatively, explore your local specialist food shops. We both live near some fantastic Vietnamese mini-markets as well as an area famous for Greek and Turkish stores. We know we'll source some key ingredients cheaper and more readily here than in large chain supermarkets. Wherever you are in the country you should be able to find shops like this, so weave them into your shopping routine whenever you get the chance.

When you're entertaining, these magic pots, jars and bottles become all the more valuable – transforming the ordinary into the extraordinary in seconds. Overleaf you will find our secret weapons.

seasonings

salt | Flaky salt crystals can be a hero ingredient in their own right, rather than just a flavour-enhancer. Sometimes we will dress a salad very simply with good oil, good salt and a splash of vinegar. Flaky salt brings out sweet notes too; try it on strawberries or peaches to intensify their flavour. Maldon smoked salt is particularly moreish; its bonfire notes are heavenly in our Salted caramel brownies (see page 229).

coloured peppercorns | Pink and green are great for rubs and marinades, and also lovely ground over ice cream with fruit, believe it or not!

oils

good-quality extra virgin olive oil | Good olive oil makes an ordinary green salad taste like a restaurant creation. It really is worth spending the extra money here; you get what you pay for. Taste and find out what you like: some people prefer the flavour of the nutty, golden oils you often find in Spain, for example, while others enjoy dark green, almost grassy, Greek oils.

British rapeseed oil | This is unflavoured, so perfect for dressings that feature other strong notes.

pistachio oil | With its beautiful emerald colour, pistachio oil adds another layer of aroma and flavour to sweet baked goods, to simple new potatoes or even your favourite dip. Although it can be more expensive than other oils, you can use it as a finishing oil to maximise its impact and make it go further; our favourite brand is La Tourangelle.

truffle oil | Truffle oil comes in a tiny bottle for a reason – it has a very powerful flavour. But it adds an inimitable extra dimension. Drizzle this on the top of a lasagne or tray-baked potatoes at the end of cooking for a rich, decadent hit.

Note: We are all in the habit of taking a bottle of wine round to someone's house when they invite us for dinner – but a bottle of good oil is such a treat for a home cook and will last and last.

hot sauces

We are both addicted to hot sauces and each of the following performs a different task with aplomb.

chipotle | This sauce is a combination of spicy hot peppers and smoky paprika. Chipotle peppers can be bought dried, then soaked in water and added to stocks or marinades. They are also available ground in a dried powder, but for a more instant hit we love to use Tabasco chipotle pepper sauce.

cholula | The 'chili lime' flavour is our favourite Cholula Hot Sauce (our friend brings it back from New York in her suitcase), but you can get the Original from most supermarkets. We drizzle this over a range of savoury dishes, from bacon sandwiches to tacos.

harissa | This Middle Eastern spice paste can be used to elevate stews, soups or couscous. We love to swirl it into yoghurt or crème fraîche for a more subtle, creamy kick, then dollop this on top of dishes, or serve it as a really simple dip with crudités. Our two most used varieties are by Belazu: rose harissa, which has lots of garlic and rose petals hidden amongst the heat of the chilli, and verbena harissa, which contains herbs and lemon for a zestier kick.

sriracha | You will have seen the green-capped Huy Fong Food Inc. bottle on the table at your local Thai or Vietnamese restaurant; it is often used as an accompaniment to noodle soups and grilled fish and meats. Sriracha is quite hot but also has a sweet and vinegary tang – we love it on avocado on toast.

spreads

butter | A simple staple for some or an investment for others, we couldn't live without good butter. Buy local from the farmers' market or use goat's butter for a more standout flavour. We love Lescure unsalted French butter, or for something salty (and more readily available), Waitrose's Brittany butter with sea salt crystals is excellent.

Note: If you're worried about food going far enough or being ready on time, great bread and butter will keep a crowd happy and full for ages. A fresh sourdough or fruit loaf and some butter (with extra salt for sprinkling) will go down a storm. Try celery salt or black salt, or lay anchovy fillets on the butter.

mustards | Mustards can add a pungent kick to otherwise mild dishes, such as a croque monsieur or cauliflower cheese, and we think Dijon mustard is a real hero here. Grainy mustard is slightly more acidic and is great for adding texture to cold cuts of meat or stirred through something smooth like mash. English is known for its sinus-clearing power but we can't resist a dollop on a cheese and tomato sandwich. Maille and Pommery are our go-to brands.

mayonnaise | We love a home-made mayo (see page 145) but sometimes shop-bought more than does the trick. It's easy to transform a simple mayo with some lemon, watercress and tarragon, or to make a speedy tartare sauce by adding capers, chopped parsley and some olive oil.

There are some really amazing mayos on the market that already have an added extra – Brindisa's Confit Garlic and Saffron mayonnaises are addictive.

sweeteners

honey | We recommend finding a local producer – honey really does taste different depending on where you live. For our summer supper club we managed to source honey from the same street where we held the dinner; the honey had subtle floral notes, which made for a perfect accompaniment to our fig panna cotta. We keep jars of clear and cloudy honey in the larder.

maple syrup | It's worth investing in quality here: always make sure it's 'pure maple syrup' from maple trees (as opposed to maple syrup that has been blended) – it costs more, but it's the real deal.

pomegranate molasses | This is great added to any Middle Eastern-style dishes, it's sweet, tangy and sticky. We love it drizzled over sweet potatoes or even hummus.

jars and tins

nuts | From koftes to rocky road (see page 106) and everything in between, nuts are the added extra in almost every J&L recipe; even the simplest dishes like roasted

vegetables or salads are transformed. Whole or chopped, toasted or roasted, we can't get enough of them. We always have a jar of hazelnuts, pistachios, walnuts and cashews to hand.

seeds | We love seeds for sweet and savoury plates. Poppy seeds are great for texture in a zesty lemon cake or for adding bite to a salad. Pumpkin seeds can be used as a crunchy topping on soups whenever friends come round or toasted with paprika for a simple and delicious snack. Fennel seeds add a subtle aniseed flavour and are great for modernising classic dishes such as celeriac rémoulade.

tinned beans | A really easy informal dinner party side dish, just add some garlic, herbs and a dollop of yoghurt to pinto, cannellini or borlotti beans. Serve with some griddled lamb or oven-roasted chicken legs. They also make the ultimate one-jar meal.

lifesaver

We always have a big tub of Total Greek-style yoghurt in the fridge for serving with desserts and for making impromptu condiments for meat, fish and vegetables. Stir in chopped dill and lemon zest, crushed garlic and paprika, ground cumin and mint – whatever you have lying around.

mexican fiesta

serves 4

micheladas
tostadas with smoked salmon,
    avocado & chipotle mayo
black bean quesadillas
skillet eggs & chorizo

Get all hands on deck for this menu: someone on tostada duty,
someone manning the egg pan, and another toasting the
quesadillas. Put all of your hot sauces out on the table so people
can choose their own.

Everywhere we went in Mexico we found *micheladas* – a take
on a Bloody Mary made with beer. They are so refreshing
we just had to include them here. Play around with the
quantities to suit your tastes, and just ramp up the chilli if you
prefer them a little hotter. This menu is also perfect if surprise
extra guests turn up, as there's always plenty to go round.

micheladas

juice of 3–4 limes (depending on how juicy they are
    and how much you like), plus extra lime wedges
about 600ml tomato juice
Worcestershire sauce, to taste
hot sauce (a Mexican sauce such as Cholula is perfect,
    but otherwise Tabasco is fine), to taste
ice cubes (loads)
4 bottles of Mexican beer (we like Pacífico, Sol or Corona)
4 shots of vodka (optional)
sea salt and black pepper

———

Pour a layer of salt on to a plate. Rub the rims of 4 tallish
tumblers with a lime wedge, then dip each tumbler rim
in the salt.

Add tomato juice to each glass to about a quarter full.
To each glass add a squeeze of lime juice, a splash of
Worcestershire sauce, a splash of hot sauce and some freshly
ground black pepper. Top up with loads of ice and add a beer
to each, with a shot of vodka if you like, and stir well. Play
around with the quantities, depending how much of each
flavour you like.

tostadas with smoked salmon, avocado & chipotle mayo

vegetable oil, for deep-frying
8 small corn tortillas (not flour ones; you can get corn tortillas
    at speciality supermarkets; the ones we use here are around
    15cm in diameter)
6 banana shallots, finely sliced into rings
4 tbsp mayonnaise (see page 145 for home-made)
2 tsp chipotle paste, harissa or any hot sauce you like
240g smoked or cured salmon, cut into thin slices
4 avocados, halved, stoned, peeled and sliced lengthways
bunch of coriander
2–3 limes, cut into wedges

———

Pour enough oil into a medium, high-sided pan, to come about a third
of the way up the sides of the pan, and heat it to 180°C.

Working in batches, deep-fry the tortillas in the hot oil for 2 minutes,
turning them every 30 seconds, until golden brown. Remove from
the oil and leave to drain on kitchen paper to absorb the excess. When
you've finished frying the tortillas, drop the oil temperature down
to 160°C and deep-fry the shallots for about 2 minutes, until golden
brown. Transfer these to clean kitchen paper to drain.

Mix the mayonnaise with the chipotle in a bowl.

To serve, top each tortilla with a slice of salmon, some slices of avocado
and a dollop of spicy mayo. Scatter over crispy shallots and coriander.
Finish with a squeeze of lime.

black bean quesadillas

2–3 tbsp olive oil
1 large white onion, finely diced
2 bunches of spring onions, finely sliced into rings
2 x 380g cartons (or tins) black beans in water, drained
2 garlic cloves, finely chopped
1 tbsp smoked paprika
8 small, soft, wheat tortillas
100g cheese, such as Cheddar (or *cotija*, if you can find it), grated

———

Heat 2 tablespoons of the oil in a pan on a low heat, add the diced onion and fry until beginning to soften, then add the spring onions. Keep an eye on them; it's good if they caramelise a little, just not too much. Remove from the pan and set aside.

Add the drained beans to the pan with a splash more oil, then add the garlic and fry until just turning golden. Add the smoked paprika and continue to fry until the beans are warmed through. Remove from the heat then briefly and roughly mash, but not to a paste; there should still be some whole beans.

Heat a ridged griddle pan until hot.

Spread a layer of bean mixture on to a tortilla, top with some onion mixture, sprinkle with cheese and top with a second tortilla, like a sandwich. Repeat with the remaining tortillas and ingredients.

Griddle the tortillas on each side until the cheese has melted and griddle lines have appeared. Cut into quarters to serve. Eat them on their own (or dip them in the skillet eggs, page 53).

skillet eggs & chorizo

1 tbsp olive oil
150g cooking chorizo, skin removed, broken into small pieces
2 jalapeños (from a jar), finely chopped
4 garlic cloves, crushed
2 x 400g tins chopped tomatoes
2 tsp caster sugar
1 tsp chipotle chilli flakes
4 eggs
60g feta, crumbled
2 large handfuls of flat-leaf parsley, roughly chopped
sea salt and black pepper
sour cream, to serve (optional)

———

Pour the olive oil into a large frying pan (25–30cm) and set over
a medium heat. Add the chorizo and cook for about 5 minutes, until
it starts to turn golden and release its fat, then add the jalapeños and
cook for a minute.

Stir in the garlic then tip in the tomatoes and turn up the heat to get
them really hot and bubbling. Add the sugar and chilli flakes. Leave
the tomatoes to bubble and lose a bit of their moisture, for about
5 minutes. Stir and season with salt and pepper to taste.

Make 4 wells in the mixture and crack an egg into the middle of each
well. Leave to cook gently until the white is solid.

Sprinkle over the feta and parsley and serve with a dollop of sour
cream on top, if you like.

weekend with friends

serves 6

grapefruit, lime & mint soda
curried avocado on toast with quick pickles
mini ricotta doughnuts with pistachios & honey
jug of iced coffee

————————

Weekend brunch at home offers plenty of benefits: no travel, unlimited table time and lots of extra helpings. Avocado on toast comes to mind immediately – if you've had it once, you've had it a million times. But we think we have hit the jackpot with our J&L version: curried avo with quick pickles that pack a punch. If you're feeling really peckish, then these ricotta doughnuts will keep you going until the early evening.

grapefruit, lime & mint soda

juice of 3 ruby or pink grapefruits
juice of 3 limes
20g mint leaves
2 x 1-litre bottles of soda or sparkling water
6 tsp runny honey

———

Mix the squeezed juices and divide between a couple of large jugs. Tear in the mint leaves and top up with the soda water. Stir 3 teaspoons of honey into each, and serve over ice.

curried avocado on toast with quick pickles

6 avocados
juice of 2 lemons, or to taste
6 tbsp extra virgin olive oil, plus extra to drizzle
3 tsp mild curry powder
6 slices of sourdough bread
sea salt and black pepper
few sprigs of coriander, to serve

for the quick pickles
1 tsp black peppercorns
1 bay leaf
200ml white wine vinegar
3 large carrots
8 radishes

———

First make the quick pickles. Put the peppercorns, bay leaf and vinegar into a pan, add 300ml water and bring to the boil. As soon as it's boiling, take off the heat and let it cool until just warm.

Meanwhile, shave the carrots and radishes into super-fine long strips (for the carrots) and rounds (for the radishes), ideally using a mandoline, or otherwise a speed peeler. Add the carrots to the pickling liquid and put to one side for 15–20 minutes. We leave our radishes raw as they add a different texture on the toast but if you want to pickle the radish too, go ahead.

Halve and stone the avocados and roughly mash them in a bowl, adding lemon juice and salt and pepper to taste, then set aside.

Mix the olive oil with the curry powder – it should have quite a loose consistency – then stir this into the avocado.

Toast your bread, then spread on the avocado mixture. Drain the pickled carrots and add to the toast with the radishes. Grind some pepper over the top, drizzle with olive oil and serve with sprigs of coriander.

mini ricotta doughnuts with pistachio & honey

185g ricotta, plus extra to serve
2 large eggs
½ teaspoon vanilla extract
90g plain flour
1 ½ tsp baking powder
1 tbsp caster sugar
pinch of salt
½ tsp ground cinnamon
vegetable oil, for frying

to coat
3 tbsp caster sugar
½ tsp ground cinnamon, or to taste

to serve
ricotta or thick yoghurt
a handful of chopped pistachios
runny honey

Beat the ricotta, eggs and vanilla extract together until smooth. Add the flour, baking powder, sugar, salt and cinnamon and continue to beat to form a batter – you want a thick 'droppable' consistency. Leave to rest for 5–10 minutes.

For the coating, mix the sugar and cinnamon together in a shallow bowl. Taste and add more cinnamon if you like.

Pour vegetable oil into a large, wide frying pan, to come to a depth of a few centimetres. Heat it to 180°C.

Use 2 teaspoons to shape rounds of batter and drop in the hot oil, making sure they aren't touching each other. Do this in about 5 batches of 5–7 doughnuts per batch – you don't want to overcrowd the pan or the temperature will drop and the doughnuts won't crisp. Fry for 3–4 minutes, until you can see a golden colour appearing on the side, turning them at this point to keep the colour even. Make sure they are cooked all the way through (remove one from the oil to test by cutting it in half), then remove and drain on kitchen paper, and repeat until the batter is used up.

Roll the warm doughnuts in the cinnamon sugar. Spoon a dollop of ricotta or yoghurt on to each plate and top with the chopped pistachios and honey. Serve with the warm doughnuts.

jug of
iced coffee

———

Make a big batch of coffee, leave
to cool then transfer to a serving
jug, add ice, agave syrup or honey
to sweeten, and top up with a milk
of your choice – we like full-fat or
hazelnut milk.

hair of the dog

serves 6

green ricotta pancakes with
   tomatoes & harissa
retox while you detox juice

———————

We don't really go in for 'healthy food' but there are certain times when we want to feel restored…usually after a night in the pub! These pancakes are best enjoyed straight away, while at their most fluffy, and are delicious with the spicy kick from the harissa. For the juice you'll need a juicer, but if that proves too noisy for a sore head, a huge pot of Yorkshire tea will surely be your saviour.

green ricotta pancakes with tomatoes & harissa

makes 18

cherry tomatoes on the vine, ideally a variety of colours
    (if you can only get red that's fine), about 4–6 per person
2 tbsp olive oil, plus extra for frying
150g baby spinach
3 large eggs, separated
150ml milk
150g plain flour
½ tsp baking powder
½ tsp bicarbonate of soda
3 spring onions, finely chopped
225g ricotta
15g flat-leaf parsley, chopped
unsalted butter, for frying
sea salt and black pepper

to serve
Greek-style yoghurt
harissa, ideally rose
extra virgin olive oil, to drizzle

———

Preheat the oven to 180°C/gas 4. Toss the tomatoes with the oil in an ovenproof dish. Sprinkle with salt and pepper then roast for 15–20 minutes, until the skins are just bursting. Remove and set aside.

Meanwhile, place a medium pan over a medium heat, then add the spinach and a little water. Cover tightly with a lid and wilt the spinach for 2–3 minutes. Drain, then once cool enough to handle, squeeze out the excess water. Pat dry and chop.

In a jug, whisk the egg yolks and milk together. Place the flour, baking powder and bicarbonate of soda in a bowl and mix well. Make a well in the centre and slowly add the egg yolk mixture, whisking until it becomes a thick batter. Add the spinach and spring onions, ricotta and parsley, season and stir until thoroughly combined.

In a separate, clean bowl, whisk the egg whites to soft peaks. Using a metal spoon, gently fold the whites one spoonful at a time into the pancake batter, trying not to lose too much air. Heat a knob of butter with a teaspoon of olive oil in a large frying pan. Place large spoonfuls of the batter in the hot pan – you can probably cook 4 pancakes at a time. Fry for about 4 minutes on each side until golden brown, then transfer to a warm platter while you cook the remaining batter. Serve in stacks of 3, topped with yoghurt and harissa. Place the warm roasted tomatoes on top and drizzle with extra virgin olive oil.

retox while you detox juice

500g kale
3 cucumbers
4 pears
4 apples (we use Granny Smiths
    for a bit of sharpness)
20cm piece of ginger
juice of 4 limes
6 shots of vodka (optional; you may not be feeling
    brave enough!)

———

Put the kale, cucumbers, pears, apples and ginger through a juicer. Add the lime juice and vodka, if using, stir well and serve immediately.

on the move

serves 6

egg muffins
banana bundts
flask of almond chai

———————

We have prepared this little care package for everything from long coastal walks with friends to dawn starts ahead of a car boot sale. Whatever the journey, it is always a morale booster to have something hearty in your backpack.

You could make the muffins and Bundts the night before, wrap them in greaseproof paper and tie with string – your companions will descend on them like seagulls. And the spicy chai is a great pick-me-up, whether you're watching the waves crash down or haggling over some china.

egg muffins

makes 6 of each flavour

for each batch of 6
5 medium eggs
5 tsp crème fraîche
sea salt and black pepper

smoked salmon, dill and spring onion
100g smoked salmon, chopped into small pieces
15g dill, chopped
4 spring onions, finely chopped

full English
6 rashers of streaky bacon, grilled until crisp then broken or chopped
    into small pieces
6 cherry tomatoes, halved
6 mushrooms, finely sliced
splash of Tabasco (optional)

———

Preheat the oven to 170°C/gas 3. Have ready a silicon muffin tray
with 6 wells, each well 7cm in diameter and 3cm deep (or use 2
trays and cook both flavours at once, doubling the egg and crème
fraîche quantities).

Mix the eggs and crème fraîche with some salt and pepper.

Divide the filling ingredients between the wells and pour in the
egg mixture until three-quarters full. Rearrange the ingredients if
everything seems to be at the bottom.

Bake for 13 minutes until just set and they have some give. Repeat
with the second flavour, if cooking in 2 batches. Eat when cooled,
or freeze and defrost as needed.

banana bundts

makes 12

150g salted butter
200g plain flour, plus extra for dusting
400g ripe bananas, peeled weight (about 4 medium)
100g soft light brown sugar
2 medium eggs
2 tsp baking powder
½ tsp bicarbonate of soda

———

Preheat the oven to 170°C/gas 3. Melt the butter in a pan over a low heat, then remove from the heat and set aside to cool. Use 2 tablespoons of the melted butter to brush the insides of a silicon mini Bundt tray, then lightly dust with flour.

Put the bananas into a bowl and mash until nearly smooth. Put the sugar and eggs into a large bowl and, using an electric whisk, beat together for 2 or 3 minutes, until well mixed and pale. Add the mashed banana and whisk again.

Sift the flour, baking powder and bicarbonate of soda into the mixture and fold in to combine.

Add the remaining melted butter and stir until fully combined. Pour the mixture into the prepared Bundt tray, leaving 1.5cm to allow room to rise. Bake for 25 minutes or until a skewer inserted into the middle comes out clean. Leave to cool in the tray.

flask of almond chai

1 litre unsweetened almond milk
6 chai tea bags (your favourite brand)

————

Warm the almond milk in a saucepan.
Remove from the heat. Add the tea bags,
cover and allow to steep for 5–7 minutes,
depending on how strong you like it.
Take the tea bags out, heat once more
and pour into flasks.

Winter Warmer

Beef California

Mash and
Roasted Sprouts

Plum and
Marzipan Brioche
Tarts

afternoon
in provence

serves 6

leg of lamb with tapenade
roasted tomatoes with white beans
strawberry mousse with lavender shortbread

———————

When people talk about a long lunch, this is what we picture
being served. It would, of course, be ideal to be sitting in
a shady courtyard outside a gîte in Provence, but we love
the charm of our own back yard too. As long as there's a glass
of wine in everyone's hand and a straw sun-hat on their head,
the scene is set.

leg of lamb
with tapenade

1 leg of lamb, with bone, about 2kg
1 whole head of garlic, cut in half across the equator
2 large carrots, halved
2 red onions, peeled and halved
2 celery sticks, halved
2 bay leaves
500ml vegetable stock

for the tapenade
2 garlic cloves, chopped
2 tbsp capers, well rinsed
1 x 30g tin anchovy fillets
160g kalamata olives, pitted
15g flat-leaf parsley, leaves only
4 tbsp olive oil
sea salt and black pepper

———

For the tapenade, put all the ingredients except the oil and seasoning into a
mini-chopper and pulse until finely chopped, then gradually pulse in the oil
until it is a thick paste. Add salt and pepper to taste.

Preheat the oven to 200°C/gas 6.

Pat dry the leg of lamb and rub half the tapenade over its surface (save the rest
for another occasion).

Pile the garlic, carrots, onions, celery and bay leaves in a roasting tin to make
a trivet for the lamb to sit on. Place the lamb on top. Add the stock and 500ml
water to the tin and roast in the oven for 30 minutes, then reduce the temperature
to 180°C/gas 4 and continue to roast for about another hour (for medium),
topping up with more water regularly if it looks dry.

When cooked to your liking, remove the lamb and vegetables and place on
a carving plate to rest. Carve and serve.

roasted tomatoes with white beans

120ml olive oil
3 anchovy fillets (in oil)
1 large banana shallot, finely chopped
1 garlic clove, halved and thinly sliced
small bunch of thyme
400ml white wine (not a very dry one)
3 x 400g tins white beans, drained (liquor reserved)
sea salt and black pepper

for the tomatoes
600g cherry tomatoes on the vine
3 tbsp olive oil
8 small sprigs of rosemary
6 small garlic cloves, cut in half lengthways

———

Preheat the oven to 200°C/gas 6. Put the tomatoes in a roasting tray or oven dish. Drizzle over the olive oil and tuck the rosemary sprigs and halved garlic cloves around the tomatoes. Cook for 20–30 minutes until the tomatoes start to char and produce juices. Sprinkle with salt and pepper to taste.

Meanwhile, put the 120ml olive oil in a large cast-iron pan over a medium heat. Add the anchovies and cook down until they have dissolved into the oil. Add the shallot and cook for about 5 minutes on a low heat, stirring occasionally and making sure it doesn't catch. Add the garlic and leave to soften briefly, then add the thyme and leave to infuse for a few minutes.

Add the wine, turn the heat up to high and bring to the boil to burn off the alcohol. Turn down to a simmer and add the beans, their reserved liquor and ½ cup of water. Cook for a further 10–15 minutes, topping up with water if it starts to dry out. Season to taste and add the roast tomatoes, stirring in the juices, then serve.

lavender shortbread

125g unsalted butter, softened
55g caster sugar, plus extra for dusting
180g plain flour
1 tsp dried lavender
pinch of salt

———

In a large mixing bowl, beat the butter and sugar together until light, creamy and smooth. Add the flour, dried lavender and salt and combine until you get a dough coming together. Tip out on to a large piece of baking parchment and shape into a rectangle about 2cm thick, in the middle of the parchment. Put another sheet of baking parchment on top and roll, to smooth and flatten to an even 1cm thickness. Slide on to a baking sheet and chill in the fridge for 30 minutes.

Remove the dough from the fridge and take off and discard the top sheet of parchment. Using a knife, score lines to go halfway through the dough, where you will want to cut into individual shortbreads. Return to the fridge and chill until hard.

Preheat the oven to 170°C/gas 3.

Bake in the oven for 20–25 minutes until the edges are starting to look dried out and biscuit-like. Remove and leave to cool down slightly for a couple of minutes, then cut through the score lines, liberally dust with sugar and leave to cool completely.

strawberry mousse

660g strawberries, hulled
225g caster sugar
sunflower oil, for greasing
5 gelatine leaves
3 large eggs, separated
2 tbsp strawberry liqueur
600ml double cream

———

Preheat the oven to 180°C/gas 4. Line a baking tray with baking parchment.

Cut 600g of the strawberries into quarters (reserving the rest whole), and spread out on the lined baking tray. Sprinkle over 75g of the sugar, followed by 2 tablespoons of water. Roast in the oven for 20 minutes, until the strawberries have dissolved and released lots of syrupy juices. Pour the syrup into a bowl and reserve, and blend the fruit in a mini-blender; you should have about 320ml purée.

Lightly oil 6 dariole moulds and line each one with a circle of baking parchment (or use one large serving bowl without the baking parchment, to be spooned rather than turned out). Thinly slice the reserved 60g strawberries and set aside. Place the gelatine leaves in a small bowl of cold water and set aside to soak.

Meanwhile, using an electric whisk, whisk the egg yolks and half the remaining sugar (i.e. 75g) in a mixing bowl, until pale and thick. Whisk in the strawberry purée and the strawberry liqueur. In another bowl, whip the cream to soft peaks and whisk briefly into the strawberry mixture, to combine.

Drain and squeeze out the gelatine leaves. Place in a small pan over a gentle heat until dissolved, then stir into the strawberry cream.

In a clean bowl, whisk the egg whites to soft peaks, then whisk in the remaining 75g sugar a tablespoon at a time. Using a metal spoon, carefully fold into the strawberry cream mixture.

Place the sliced strawberries in the base(s) of the prepared mould(s), then top up with the mousse mixture and place in the fridge to set, for at least 3 hours and ideally overnight.

To serve, dip each mould briefly in warm water. Put a plate on top, flip over and shake lightly – it should plop out. Serve the mousse(s) with the reserved syrup and lavender shortbread (see page 85).

catch
of the day

serves 6

fried artichoke hearts with cannellini beans,
   parmesan & aïoli
brown paper trout
coconut & honey bundt
no-churn ricotta ice cream

———————

Large sharing plates epitomise our no-fuss sharing ethos,
but sometimes it's really special to serve something individual.
Steaming fish in parcels 'en papillote', as the French say,
means that each guest can have their own present to unwrap,
and the scent is beautiful when it's opened. Try the parcels
using whatever tickles your fancy at the fishmonger; a few clams
or mussels thrown in with the fish would be a great flavour
injection too.

fried artichoke hearts with cannellini beans, parmesan & aïoli

2 x 290g jars artichoke hearts in olive oil
   (about 400g total artichoke weight)
3 tbsp olive oil
1 tsp dried chilli flakes, or more for extra heat
2 x 400g tins cannellini beans (other white
   beans also work well), drained
20g piece of Parmesan
drizzle of extra virgin olive oil
10–20 basil leaves (regular or purple)

for the aïoli
½ small garlic clove
1 medium egg yolk
200ml olive oil
juice of ½ lemon, or more to taste
½ tsp Dijon mustard
sea salt and black pepper

———

Start by making the aïoli. Using the flat side of a large knife, crush the garlic to a paste with a little salt (this helps the garlic to break down) and set aside.

Place the egg yolk in a clean bowl, with a damp tea towel under the bowl to keep it steady. Using a balloon whisk, lightly whisk the yolk, then start to whisk in the oil a few drops at a time – this might seem slow but we have had so many 'mayo splits' that it's worth taking your time to get it right. Adding a few drops of lemon juice as you go also helps keep it more stable and less likely to split. After each addition of oil, make sure it is all combined before adding the next, whisking continuously until the mixture becomes thick and 'mayo-like'. Continue until all the oil has been used.

Add the lemon juice; this will loosen up the mixture. Add the mustard and the garlic paste. Add salt and pepper to taste and, if you prefer a bit more zing, add more lemon juice. Set aside.

Drain the artichokes from their oil; you still want a bit of oil coating them, for frying. Put the hearts into a frying pan over a medium heat and fry for about 3 minutes on each side, until crispy and golden, then transfer to a plate and set aside.

Place the frying pan back over a medium heat and add the olive oil and chilli flakes. Let the oil infuse for a couple of minutes, just until the chilli starts to colour, then add the drained cannellini beans so they warm through. Add 3 tablespoons of water and keep stirring until the mixture thickens into a creamy sort of sauce. Add the artichokes and cook everything together for a further 2 minutes. Pour the bean mixture into a serving bowl, spoon over some aïoli, very finely grate over the Parmesan (we use a Microplane), drizzle with extra virgin olive oil and scatter over the basil leaves to serve.

brown paper trout

900g baby new potatoes, scrubbed
300g samphire
6 trout fillets, 150g each
1 lemon, thinly sliced
60g capers, well rinsed and roughly chopped
30g chives, finely chopped
30g dill, finely chopped
olive oil, for drizzling
sea salt and black pepper

———

Preheat the oven to 200°C/gas 6. Cut out 6 pieces of greaseproof paper, each 40cm square, and set aside.

Boil the potatoes in salted water until *al dente*, then drain and leave to cool a little before cutting into slices about the thickness of a pound coin.

In the centre of each square of greaseproof paper, pile up equal amounts of samphire and potatoes. Add a trout fillet to each, then top with the lemon slices, capers, herbs and then a drizzle of oil. Sprinkle with salt and pepper, bearing in mind that the samphire and capers are salty.

Seal the parcel by folding over the edges of the greaseproof paper all the way along, making sure there is plenty of space between the ingredients and the sealed edge for air to circulate during cooking. Place on a baking tray and cook in the oven for about 12 minutes. Let each person open their own parcel.

coconut & honey bundt

125g unsalted butter, plus extra for greasing
200g plain flour, plus extra for dusting
180g caster sugar
3 large eggs
4 tbsp floral runny honey, plus extra to serve
finely grated zest of 1 lemon
160g coconut-flavoured yoghurt,
    or Greek-style yoghurt with coconut
25g desiccated coconut
1 ½ tsp baking powder
pinch of salt

———————

Preheat the oven to 180°C/gas 4. Butter and lightly flour a 26-cm Bundt tin.

Cream the butter and sugar together until light, fluffy and pale. Add the eggs, one at a time, only adding the next egg when the previous one is combined.

Add the honey, lemon zest, yoghurt and desiccated coconut, and stir to combine.

Sift in the flour, baking powder and salt and combine to make a batter. Pour into the prepared Bundt tin and level the surface with a spatula.

Bake in the oven for 45–50 minutes, until cooked through. To check, insert a skewer into the middle: if it comes out clean, it's ready. If the skewer is sticky, give the cake another 3–5 minutes before checking again.

Remove from the oven and leave to cool in the tin for at least 30 minutes, then turn out on to a cooling rack to finish cooling, or serve still warm with a scoop of ricotta ice cream and a drizzle of honey.

no-churn
ricotta ice cream

(serves 6, so double the quantities if you want
   enough over to go with the leftover Bundt)

3 tbsp floral runny honey
1 ½ tbsp vanilla extract
220g ricotta
200ml double cream

———

In a bowl, mix together the honey, vanilla, ricotta and 50ml of the
cream, then set aside.

In a separate bowl, whisk the remaining 150ml cream until soft
peaks form. Fold the ricotta mixture into the whipped cream until
fully combined.

Transfer to a tin and cover with cling film, or use a plastic container
with a lid. Put in the freezer for 4 hours and take out a few minutes
before you want to serve.

rooftop picnic

serves 6

cheese & chive dip
chicken & pesto loaf sandwich
tomato, feta & thyme tart
white chocolate, sour cherry
   & pistachio rocky road

————————

Living in the city we crave open spaces, so when the temperature is a notch above zero we race to eat our meals outside. All four of these recipes are showstoppers in their own right (if only for their ease of preparation: the loaf sandwich can be made the day before the picnic and the rocky road up to a week ahead of time). Grab a basket and blanket, and find a patch of dappled light in the park, or even better, a rooftop with a view.

cheese & chive dip

3 tbsp olive oil
100g spring onions (about 2 very large ones), trimmed
    and thinly sliced
1 garlic clove, crushed
25g chives, finely chopped
250g Greek yoghurt
40g Gruyère, finely grated (we use a Microplane)
1 red onion, finely sliced into rings
smoked salt and white pepper

to serve
good extra virgin olive oil
favourite raw vegetables, cut into batons or florets, to serve

———

Heat 1 tablespoon of the oil in a frying pan over a medium heat,
add the spring onions with a pinch of smoked salt and fry until
just beginning to caramelise, for about 5 or 6 minutes. Lower the
heat, add the garlic and cook for a minute or so more; watch it
carefully so as not to let the garlic burn.

Remove from the heat and stir in all but a handful of the chives,
reserving these for a garnish. Tip the yoghurt into your serving
bowl and stir in the spring onion and chive mixture with the
grated cheese, until thoroughly combined. Add a splash or two
of water depending on how thick you like your dip, and some
white pepper. Chill until ready to serve.

Heat the remaining 2 tablespoons of oil in the same frying pan,
add the red onion and fry until crispy. When it starts to catch
and brown, remove from the heat and sprinkle with a pinch of
smoked salt.

To serve, drizzle the yoghurt with good olive oil and top with
the fried red onion and reserved chives. Serve with crudités.

chicken & pesto loaf sandwich

2 large beetroots, trimmed
drizzle of olive oil
2 red peppers
2 yellow peppers
1 large cob or 'boule' loaf
3 tbsp pesto
4 large confit garlic cloves (see page 156),
    mashed to a purée
50g rocket
200g buffalo mozzarella, sliced and well drained
150g shredded roast chicken
sea salt and black pepper

———

Preheat the oven to 180°C/gas 4. Rub a drizzle of olive oil over the beetroots and wrap each one in foil. Cook in the oven for around an hour, until a skewer goes easily in and out. Remove and set aside to cool. Increase the oven temperature to 220°C/gas 7.

Put the peppers on a foil-lined baking sheet or tray. Roast for about 25 minutes, turning once, until the skins are blackened. Take out of the oven and carefully, using tongs, put them straight into a food bag. Tie the bag to create steam inside. When they are cool enough to handle (but not cold, as peeling gets harder), peel off the blackened skins and remove the seeds. Tear the flesh into strips. Peel and thinly slice the cooled beetroots.

Slice the top off the loaf; this will be your lid. Carefully scoop out most of the doughy insides (make into breadcrumbs and freeze), trying not to damage the sides of the loaf. Spread the pesto all over the insides of the loaf, base and sides. Spread the confit garlic paste on the underside of the lid.

Layer half the rocket into the base, then a layer of mozzarella. Add half the roasted pepper strips, then half the chicken, then half the beetroot slices. Add a little seasoning and press down gently to start compressing the layers, and to make more room.

Repeat the layering process, ending with a layer of beetroot, and place the lid back on. Wrap tightly in cling film and refrigerate.

On picnic day, bring the loaf to room temperature and take the whole thing with you. To serve, either slice or cut into wedges like a cake.

tomato, feta
& thyme tart

butter, for greasing
375g all-butter shortcrust pastry
3 medium eggs
200ml double cream
12 thyme sprigs, leaves picked
125g soft goat's cheese
150g feta, crumbled into small bits
400g cherry tomatoes, a mix of colours and varieties, halved
sea salt and black pepper

———

Preheat the oven to 200°C/gas 6. Lightly grease a deep, fluted, 25-cm, loose-based tart tin.

Roll out the pastry to the size of the tin with enough to hang over the edges. Lay the pastry in the tin and gently press it into the edges and ridges of the tin. Prick a few times over the base with a fork.

Put a large sheet of baking parchment on top of the pastry, so it has a large overhang, and fill with baking beans. Blind bake for 15 minutes, then carefully remove the paper and the beans and bake for 5 minutes more, until golden. Remove from the oven, trim away the overhanging pastry and set aside to cool while you make the filling.

Mix the eggs, cream and thyme leaves with some salt and pepper, then add the goat's cheese. Use a whisk to mix it all, breaking the goat's cheese up so it's not in huge lumps. Pour the mixture into the pastry case.

Sprinkle the feta evenly over the tart and arrange the tomatoes, cut side up and in concentric circles, pushing them down gently so they don't sit proud of the liquid. Bake for 25 minutes, until the filling mixture is set and turning golden in places.

white chocolate, sour cherry & pistachio rocky road

makes 15 squares

400g good-quality white chocolate
20g pink marshmallows, roughly chopped
60g shortbread biscuits, roughly chopped
30g desiccated coconut
10g plain popcorn
60g shelled unsalted pistachios
110g dried cherries

———

Line a baking tin, 26 x 17cm, with cling film.

Melt the chocolate in a heatproof bowl set over a pan of boiling water over a low heat, making sure that the water doesn't touch the bottom of the bowl.

While the chocolate is melting, put the chopped marshmallows and shortbread in a bowl and add the coconut, popcorn, pistachios and dried cherries. Mix well.

When the chocolate has melted, remove it from the heat and leave to cool before adding to the dry mixture and mixing thoroughly.

Tip the mixture into the lined tin, spreading out to the edges, and refrigerate for 2 hours until firm. Remove from the fridge, lift out of the tin and cut into 15 squares. Store in an airtight container in the fridge for up to a week.

easter gathering

serves 6–8

slow-roasted shoulder of lamb
  with anchovy sauce
boulangère potatoes
aubergine gratin
broccoli with hazelnuts
rhubarb crumble pots

————————

We've called this an Easter gathering because it reminds us of the Bank Holiday weekend back home, when the sun is desperately trying to warm up the garden and the house is full of people. But this is perfect for any spring day when you can get everyone together. The lamb should stay warm while you cook the potatoes and aubergines; just keep it tightly covered with foil. Feel free to substitute the rhubarb pots for a big shard of cracked milk chocolate from your pile of eggs!

slow-roasted shoulder of lamb with anchovy sauce

1 shoulder of lamb, with bone (about 2kg)
8 short rosemary sprigs
8 anchovy fillets in oil, plus the oil from the tin
olive oil
sea salt and black pepper

———

Preheat your oven to 220°C/gas 7.

With a sharp knife, pierce 8 deep incisions into the lamb at regular intervals. Stab a rosemary sprig through the middle of an anchovy and stuff the whole thing into the hole, pushing it down so the anchovy wraps around each side of the sprig and so that the sprig sits under the meat in between the layers of fat. Pour the oil from the anchovy tin over the meat and season lightly.

Roast in the oven for 30 minutes, then reduce the oven setting to 160°C/gas 3 and roast for another 3 hours, until the fat has turned golden brown and the meat is falling away from the bone. Remove from the oven and increase the oven temperature to 170°C/gas 3. Cover the lamb in foil and leave to rest while you cook the potatoes and aubergines.

boulangère potatoes

80g unsalted butter, plus a little melted for brushing
1 tbsp olive oil
4 large onions, thinly sliced
1.5kg floury potatoes, Vivaldi variety
    (or King Edward if you can't find Vivaldi),
    sliced 3mm thick
a few thyme sprigs
500ml hot chicken stock (homemade or good-
    quality shop-bought)
sea salt and black pepper

———

Use 20g of the butter to grease the base and sides of an ovenproof dish 35 x 24cm and 6cm deep.

Heat 40g of the remaining butter with the olive oil in a large frying pan on a low heat. Add the onions and cook until soft but not coloured, for about 15–20 minutes. Remove from the heat.

Add a layer of potatoes to the buttered dish, then sprinkle with salt and pepper (go easy with the salt). Add a layer of onions and some thyme and repeat with two more layers. Finish with a final layer of potatoes and press down so that all the layers make contact. Pour the hot stock evenly over the top and season again. Dot the surface with the remaining 20g butter.

Cover the dish tightly with foil and cook in the oven at 170°C/gas 3 for 1 hour until the potatoes are soft. Remove from the oven, take off the foil and increase the oven temperature to 220°C/gas 7. Brush the surface with melted butter and return to the oven. Cook for a further 20–25 minutes, until the potatoes on top are crisp and golden.

aubergine gratin

2 large white onions, thinly sliced
4 tbsp olive oil
2 garlic cloves, finely chopped
2 large aubergines, sliced lengthways into 5mm slices
400ml double cream
75g pecorino or Parmesan, grated
sea salt and black pepper

―――――

Cook the onions in a splash of the olive oil over a medium heat, until softened. Add the garlic and fry for 30 seconds, then remove from the heat and transfer to a small ovenproof dish.

Meanwhile, heat a ridged griddle pan over a medium heat. Lightly brush one side of each aubergine slice with oil and place, oiled side down, in the griddle pan, in batches. Grill until charred, then lightly brush the top sides with oil and remove to a plate, stacking them up as you cook the rest; this will help them to continue cooking and soak up the oil.

Gently heat the cream to warm it through. Layer the aubergine slices on top of the onions, adding salt and pepper between each layer. Pour the cream over the aubergines, scatter over the grated cheese and place in the oven 15 minutes after the potatoes have gone in, at 170°C/gas 3. Cook for 45 minutes, then remove while the potatoes finish cooking at the higher temperature. The aubergines should be completely silky and softened and the top golden. Cover with foil for the last few minutes if it's browning too quickly.

broccoli with hazelnuts

400g Tenderstem or purple sprouting broccoli
50g hazelnuts
2 tbsp olive oil
freshly grated nutmeg, to taste
flaky sea salt

―――――

Boil the broccoli for 3 minutes, until just tender. Drain and rinse with cold water to stop the cooking. Toast the hazelnuts in a dry frying pan until fragrant and lightly toasted, then remove from the pan and set aside.

Add a tablespoon of the oil to the frying pan over a medium heat. Add the broccoli and hazelnuts to the pan and lightly fry until mixed and the broccoli has warmed through. Drizzle with the remaining oil, sprinkle with flaky salt and grate over some nutmeg to serve.

rhubarb crumble pots

for the rhubarb
600g rhubarb, cut into 5-cm lengths (the size
    depends on the width and shape of your
    serving glasses or dishes)
1 vanilla pod, split lengthways, seeds
    scraped out
juice of 1 orange, plus 3 strips of pared rind
120g caster sugar

for the crumble topping
85g unsalted butter, diced
225g plain flour
100g soft light brown sugar

for the bottom layer
80g vanilla mini marshmallows, chopped
zest of ½ lemon, plus juice of 1 lemon
150g whipping cream
150g Greek yoghurt

Preheat the oven to 110°C/gas ¼.

Arrange the rhubarb in an ovenproof dish large enough to hold it in a single layer. Add the vanilla pod and seeds and the strips of orange rind. Sprinkle the sugar evenly over the rhubarb and then pour over the orange juice. Cover tightly with foil and cook in the oven for 2 hours. Remove from the oven and leave undisturbed in the dish until completely cold. Chill, reserving the juices separately.

Increase the oven temperature to 190°C/gas 5. Line a baking tray with baking parchment. For the crumble topping, rub the butter into the flour until it resembles breadcrumbs, then mix in the sugar. Sprinkle with a little water and, using your hands, bring some of the mixture together to create small lumps (this way the finished topping will be more crunchy). Spread the mixture out on the baking tray and cook in the oven for about 20 minutes, until golden. Remove from the oven, break it up a little and leave on the tray to cool. (This will keep in an airtight container or in the freezer; any extra is handy to add to desserts.)

Put the marshmallows and lemon zest and juice in a non-stick saucepan over a low heat to melt. Keep an eye on them and give them a stir to stop them scorching on the bottom of the pan. Once melted, remove from the heat and set aside to cool. Whip the cream slowly into soft peaks that just begin to hold their shape. Gently fold in the yoghurt followed by the melted, cooled marshmallow mixture (this stage can be done the day before).

To assemble, swirl the reserved rhubarb juices through the marshmallow and yoghurt mixture and spoon into individual serving glasses or bowls. Place in the fridge for at least 2 hours to set. To serve, add a layer of rhubarb to each and scatter over the crumble.

last barbecue of the year

serves 6

smoky barbecued corn
jewelled couscous
pistachio koftas with harissa yoghurt
summer coleslaw
grilled pineapple, chilli, mint
   & crème fraîche

———————

There is that final day of the summer when the sun shines miraculously bright, even though autumn is just around the corner. That's the day we squeeze out every last drop of the season and bare-ankle weather by getting everyone over for the last barbecue of the year. The £5 disposable barbecue, once seen as fit only for burgers and bangers, is now an essential bit of kit for any home cook. With limited space in the city you can cook up an entire feast – just be careful of those eyebrows (we speak from experience). Get the barbecue on in plenty of time, ideally 30–45 minutes before you start cooking – you want the coals to have a red glow with a fine coating of ash.

smokey barbecued corn

6 whole corn cobs, husks removed
3 tbsp mayonnaise
juice of 1 lime
1 tbsp chilli powder
50g Parmesan, finely grated
1 tbsp smoked paprika
small handful of coriander, finely chopped
sea salt and black pepper

———

Get the barbecue heating up.

Boil your corn in a pan of boiling water over a medium heat for 5–15 minutes, until cooked (the timing will depend on how young and tender the corn is). Drain and place on the hot barbecue. Rotate until evenly charred.

In a bowl, mix the mayonnaise, lime juice and chilli powder. Spread this mixture over the charred cobs, coating them evenly in a thin layer.

Scatter the Parmesan, smoked paprika and some salt and pepper on a baking tray and roll each of the mayo-coated corns thoroughly in the mixture to coat.

Sprinkle with a little coriander and serve. Have some napkins at the ready as it can be messy!

jewelled
couscous

400g couscous
50ml olive oil
250g ripe tomatoes
3 spring onions, sliced
juice of 1 lemon
½ tsp ground allspice
20g coriander
20g mint
50g flat-leaf parsley
sea salt and black pepper

––––––

Put the couscous in a heatproof bowl, add a teaspoon of the olive oil and stir it in so all the grains are coated. Cover the couscous with boiling water so the grains are just submerged, cover the bowl with a tea towel and set aside for 5 minutes.

Dice the tomatoes and tip into a bowl with any juices from dicing them. Add the spring onions, lemon juice and allspice and mix together.

Pick the herb leaves off the stalks, wash and finely chop (discard the stalks). Add the herbs to the tomato bowl.

Fluff up the couscous with a fork and add to the tomatoes and herbs with the remaining olive oil. Season to taste and mix well.

pistachio koftas
& harissa yoghurt

½ tsp fennel seeds
½ tsp coriander seeds
900g lamb shoulder, roughly diced (or you can use minced lamb)
pinch of hot paprika
½ tsp sumac
1 garlic clove, crushed
45g pistachios, roughly chopped
sea salt and black pepper
6 pitta breads, to serve

for the harissa yoghurt
170g plain yoghurt
1 tsp sumac
2 tsp harissa paste or chilli sauce

———

Soak 12 wooden skewers in cold water. Toast the fennel and coriander seeds in a small, dry frying pan for a few minutes until they become fragrant, then transfer to a pestle and mortar and crush.

Add the crushed seeds to a food processor with the diced lamb, paprika, sumac, garlic, pistachios and some salt and pepper. Pulse for a few seconds until the meat has minced. (If using minced lamb, just mix it all together in a bowl using your hands.)

Drain and dry the skewers then, using your hands, mould the meat mixture into little sausage (kofta) shapes around each skewer. Put them on a plate, then in the fridge to chill and firm up for 30 minutes until you are ready to barbecue.

Meanwhile, for the harissa yoghurt, mix all the ingredients together in a bowl, with seasoning to taste. Set aside in the fridge until ready to serve.

Cook the koftas on the barbecue for around 10 minutes, turning halfway so they are evenly cooked. Grill the pitta on the barbecue, or toast them, and serve the koftas with the pitta and harissa yoghurt alongside.

summer coleslaw

2 fennel bulbs, trimmed
1 red cabbage
150g radishes, trimmed
4 carrots, peeled
juice of 1 lemon
1 bunch of spring onions, finely
    sliced
10–15g mint leaves
10–15g coriander leaves
10–15g parsley leaves
8 tbsp plain yoghurt
1 tsp dried chilli flakes
sea salt and black pepper
handful of chopped walnuts and/
    or pomegranate seeds, to serve

———

Using a mandoline or a very
sharp knife, finely slice the fennel,
cabbage, radishes and carrots.
Place in a large serving bowl and
squeeze over the lemon juice.
Add the spring onions.

Finely chop all the herbs and add
to the bowl. Mix in the yoghurt
and season to taste. Sprinkle over
the chilli flakes and mix one final
time. Scatter over the walnuts
and/or pomegranate seeds
before serving.

grilled pineapple with chilli, mint & crème fraîche

1 ½ medium-ripe pineapples (to give a quarter per person)
juice of 3 limes
splash of rum (for a boozy kick; optional!)
100g brown sugar
1 tsp dried chilli flakes
small handful of mint leaves, finely chopped
crème fraîche, to serve

———

Cut the whole pineapple into quarters and the half pineapple in half (so you have 6 pieces), leaving the leaves on – not only does this look pretty, but it's functional, too, as you can use the leaves as a handle.

Squeeze the lime juice over the flesh, and splash over the rum, if using. Sprinkle the brown sugar into a baking tray or on to a plate and press the pineapple down into it so that it sticks to the flesh.

Transfer the pineapple quarters to the barbecue and grill for a couple of minutes on each cut side, until the sugar has caramelised. Slice each quarter horizontally so that it's easier to eat, sprinkle with the chilli flakes and mint and serve with a dollop of crème fraîche.

low & slow

serves 6

pulled pork shoulder
   & baked sweet potatoes
crunchy fennel salad with cashew & orange
almond brioche bread & butter pudding

––––––––

This is a messy, sticky, charred endeavour; one for picking
and pulling at. The salads provide a much-needed bite
and freshness and the pudding is the definition of comfort.
Blustery day and open fire optional.

pulled pork shoulder
& baked sweet potatoes

3.5–4kg shoulder of pork,
 bone in, skin on
1 onion, sliced into thick
 rings
2 celery sticks, quartered
½ garlic bulb, cloves
 separated and left
 unpeeled
1 lemon (or the leftover
 skins from the marinade
 lemon)
500ml dry white wine
6 medium-sized sweet
 potatoes
olive oil, for rubbing
sea salt and black pepper

for the marinade
1 ½ tsp cumin seeds
2 tsp smoked paprika
2 tsp sea salt
½ tsp pepper
6 garlic cloves, peeled
juice of 1 lemon

———

To prepare the marinade, toast the cumin seeds in a dry frying pan on a low heat, shaking the pan occasionally. You should start to smell the aromatics as they toast and, once slightly coloured, take them off the heat. In a pestle and mortar grind the seeds to a fine powder, then add the smoked paprika, salt, pepper, garlic and lemon juice (keep the lemon skins for the pork if you like) and pound into a sticky paste. Massage the marinade into the sides and underside of the pork, keeping the skin side clean. Cover with foil and marinate in the fridge for at least 2 hours, or overnight if possible.

Preheat the oven to 220°C/gas 7. Take the meat out the fridge half an hour before cooking to bring it to room temperature. Score the skin of the pork in a criss-cross pattern, with the lines around 1–2cm apart, without cutting down into the meat (if unsure, ask your butcher to do this beforehand). Season with a good pinch of salt, making sure you get it into the scores.

Put the onion, celery and garlic in a large roasting tray. Quarter the lemon (or reserved lemon skins) and add to the vegetables. Sit your pork, skin side up, comfortably on top. Add the wine to the tray, making sure you don't pour it over the skin, as you want that dry to help the crackling crackle.

Pop in the oven on the middle shelf and roast for 30 minutes to allow the skin to start its crackle. Whip the pork out and cover the tray tightly with thick foil (we like to put a few layers over it both length- and width-ways, to keep it tucked in). Reduce the oven temperature to 150°C/gas 2 and roast for another 4 ½ hours.

Towards the end of the cooking time, prepare your sweet potatoes by rubbing them all over with olive oil. Place on a baking tray and season well.

Take the pork out of the oven, remove the foil and baste the meat (avoiding the skin). Put the oven temperature up again to 200°C/gas 6 and return it to the oven, along with the sweet potatoes. Roast for 15–20 minutes more, to give the crackling a final blast, then take out and allow to rest while you make the fennel salad, leaving the sweet potatoes in the oven for 10–15 minutes more, or until soft.

To serve, remove the crackling and break it up into pieces. Use a fork to pull the pork meat into shreds, and serve with the sweet potatoes and fennel salad.

crunchy fennel salad with cashew & orange

2 oranges
1 fennel bulb
small pinch of sea salt
500g broad beans in pods, or 200g frozen if not in season
70g cashew nuts
60g rocket
25g mint, roughly chopped
good glug of extra virgin olive oil
juice of ½ lemon

———

Using a sharp knife, slice just the ends off both oranges. Stand one on its end and use the knife to remove the zest, pith and outer membranes, cutting from top to bottom and following the contour of the orange. Repeat with the second orange, then slice both peeled oranges into rounds. Cut the rounds into half moons and place in a serving bowl.

Trim off the fennel end and slightly fibrous tops (you can keep any thin sprigs growing amongst its stems to add to the salad later). Thinly slice, ideally with a mandoline, and add to the oranges with the salt.

Pod the broad beans, if using fresh, and add to a small pan of boiling water, then take off the heat and leave for 3–4 minutes (this loosens the bitter skins and makes them easier to remove). Drain and slip the beans out of their skins.

Lightly toast the cashews in a frying pan on a low heat, shaking the pan occasionally to avoid them catching. When lightly browned, take off the heat and tip on to a plate.

Add the skinned beans, rocket and half the cashews and mint to the oranges and fennel. Lightly toss with the olive oil and lemon juice and sprinkle the remaining cashews and mint on top.

almond brioche bread
& butter pudding

35g unsalted butter,
  softened, plus extra for
  greasing
25g almond nut butter
400g brioche loaf, cut into
  slices about 1.5cm thick
6 medium eggs
500ml unsweetened
  almond milk
2 tsp ground cinnamon
1 tbsp demerara sugar
50g flaked almonds,
  toasted

for the vanilla custard
250ml double cream
250ml whole milk
1 vanilla pod, split in half
  lengthways and seeds
  scraped
5 medium egg yolks
75g caster sugar

Preheat the oven to 180°C/gas 4. Grease a large, deep baking dish with butter.

In a bowl, mix the butter with the almond nut butter, then lightly spread over one side of each brioche slice. Cut each piece diagonally into 2 triangles.

Crack the eggs into a bowl and lightly whisk. Add the almond milk and one teaspoon of the cinnamon and whisk together well with a balloon whisk. Take a piece of the buttered brioche and dunk it into the egg and almond milk mixture, submerging it completely but briefly, then place in the prepared baking dish. Repeat with the remaining slices, arranging them in overlapping layers. Pour over the remaining egg and almond milk mixture a little at a time, letting it absorb into the bread for a minute or two between additions. Stop when you can just see it up the sides and the points of the brioche are still visible; you may not need to use it all.

Mix the demerara sugar, remaining teaspoon of cinnamon and the toasted flaked almonds together and scatter evenly over the top of the pudding. Place the dish on a baking sheet (in case it bubbles over) and bake in the oven on the middle shelf for 40 minutes, until golden brown with crispy top and edges – if it is still looking wet in the middle, pop it back in for another 5–10 minutes. Allow it to rest for 10 minutes.

Meanwhile, to make the custard, place the cream, milk, vanilla pod and seeds in a medium saucepan. Over a low heat, bring just up to simmering (don't boil it) then remove from the heat. Whisk the egg yolks and sugar in a large bowl. Slowly pour in the hot cream mixture and whisk well. Rinse out the pan then pour the egg and cream mixture into it and put back over a medium heat. Whisk constantly until the custard starts to thicken – once it starts, it will go quite quickly. Don't cook it for too long or you'll end up with something more like scrambled egg. Once thickened, remove from the heat and pour through a sieve into a clean bowl or jug. Give it a last whisk and it's ready to serve with the bread and butter pudding. (If you make the custard in advance, cover the surface with cling film to stop a skin forming.)

Winter Warmer

Beef California

Mash and
Roasted Sprouts

Plum and
Marzipan Brioche
Tarts

winter warmer

serves 6

beef california with mashed potato
   & roast sprouts
plum & marzipan brioche tarts

———————

Alice's mum has been making this slow beef for years and
everyone always immediately demands the recipe. The same
tatty instruction sheet has been copied so many times that no
one can quite remember the changes and additions that have
been made along the way – we think the original version was
a Valentina Harris recipe. In short, this is a hot-water bottle
of a menu. Rich, saucy, satisfying and best served after a walk
so cold it has turned your cheeks pink. Pop the meat in the
oven before you leave the house and come home to a melt-in-
the-mouth dish; you can cut the beef with a spoon.

beef california with mashed potatoes & roast sprouts

50g unsalted butter
2 or 3 small shallots, finely
    diced
1.5-kg piece of beef
    silverside
3 tbsp plain flour
small wine glass of red
    wine vinegar
400ml meat stock (home-
    made is best, or use a
    good-quality fresh one)
400ml single cream
sea salt and black pepper

for the roast sprouts
500g Brussels sprouts
olive oil, for drizzling

for the mash
1kg Desiree potatoes,
    peeled and cut into
    thumb-length chunks
1 bunch of spring onions,
    ends trimmed
200ml whole milk
75g unsalted butter

Preheat the oven to 170°C/gas 3. Melt the butter in a cast-iron ovenproof pan (or flameproof casserole) that has a lid, add the shallots and fry for 5 minutes. Scoop out with a slotted spoon and set aside.

Dust the piece of beef with flour, then brown on all sides in the butter. To avoid the sauce being bitter, remove the browned meat to a dish and wipe out any burned flour. Turn the heat up high and pour in the vinegar.

Once the vinegar has evaporated, add the stock and cream. Season with salt and pepper, then return the shallots and meat to the pan. Cover with a lid and transfer to the oven for 3 hours, turning it every so often to make sure it cooks evenly. It is done when the meat is very tender and yields to pressure from a couple of forks. Remove and keep warm while you make the mash and sprouts.

Increase the oven temperature to 200°C/gas 6.

Toss the sprouts in enough olive oil to coat, spread out in a roasting tin and roast for 35–45 minutes, until crispy on the outside and soft and pulpy inside.

Meanwhile, bring plenty of salted water to the boil (enough to cover the potatoes easily), add the potatoes and cook for 15–20 minutes until really soft – a knife should slide in very easily (better overdone than underdone).

While the potatoes are boiling, arrange the spring onions in an oven tray in a single layer with a drizzle of oil and a sprinkle of salt. Cook in the oven alongside the sprouts for about 15 minutes, until completely soft and the dark green ends are starting to go brown. Remove to a plate or board.

Drain and rice the potatoes, if you have a ricer, otherwise use a potato masher. Warm the milk and the butter together in a pan over a low heat just until the butter has melted; don't let it boil. Add half the milk mixture to the potato and use a spoon to combine it all, then keep adding the mixture until you have the consistency you like. We like quite a wet mash.

If necessary, reheat the beef for a few minutes in the hot oven or on the hob, then serve with the sprouts and the mash topped with the spring onions.

plum & marzipan brioche tarts

6 slices of brioche, each 2.5cm thick
about 70g softened butter, for spreading
30g soft light brown sugar, plus a little extra to finish
6 plums (they don't have to be ripe), depending
    on size, stoned and each cut into 4–6 wedges
40g marzipan, cut into 1-cm cubes
icing sugar, to dust

———————

Preheat the oven to 190°C/gas 5. Line a baking tray with baking parchment.

Spread both sides and all the edges of the brioche slices with the softened butter.

Place the sugar in a shallow bowl and dip each slice in the sugar to coat on every side. Place the coated slices on the lined tray. Arrange 4–6 wedges of plum on each slice of brioche, with the wedges overlapping each other slightly. Scatter the marzipan pieces over the plums. Sprinkle over a little more sugar.

Bake in the oven for 15–20 minutes, watching them carefully so they don't burn (if the plums are under-ripe the tarts may take a little longer).

Remove from the oven and immediately transfer from the baking tray to a cooling rack (if you leave them on the tray the bases may go soft). Serve hot or cold, and all temperatures in between, dusted with icing sugar.

boxing day grazing

serves 6

crunchy kohlrabi, radish & dill salad
maple & honey roast ham with watercress
celeriac & fennel seed rémoulade
chocolate & ginger cake with sherry buttercream

Christmas time, possibly one of our favourite times of year – the season of the elasticised waistband, cosy nights and box sets. We love the feast on the big day but there is nothing like stretching out the party by inviting the gang over to celebrate Boxing Day, too. Any leftovers (wishful thinking!) will make the perfect filling for a doorstep sandwich.

crunchy kohlrabi, radish & dill salad

1 kohlrabi, peeled and cut in half
small bunch of radishes, trimmed
1 fennel bulb, trimmed
2 avocados
few mint sprigs, leaves picked
bunch of dill, leaves picked
200g feta
6 slices of sourdough bread

for the dressing
2 tbsp olive oil
about 1 tbsp lemon juice, or more to taste
few drops of truffle oil (optional)
sea salt and black pepper

───────

Ideally using a mandoline, shave the kohlrabi halves, radishes and fennel into really thin slices, then add to a bowl.

Halve the avocados, remove the stone, scoop out the flesh and roughly chop (this doesn't need precision – messy is best). Add to the bowl.

Roughly chop the mint and dill, crumble the feta and add these to the bowl.

Make the dressing by whisking all the ingredients together, adding the lemon juice and salt and pepper to taste, and the truffle oil if you're feeling luxurious. Lightly dress the salad and leave to stand while you griddle the bread, lightly toasting it on both sides.

This is best served in the bowl for everyone to share, or piled high on individual plates with a side of the toast.

celeriac & fennel seed rémoulade

2 tbsp fennel seeds
1 medium celeriac
juice of 1 lemon
2½ tbsp mayonnaise (good-quality shop-bought
   or home-made)
1 tbsp Greek yoghurt
2 tbsp Dijon mustard
large bunch of flat-leaf parsley, chopped
sea salt and black pepper

for the home-made mayonnaise
1 medium egg yolk
200ml olive oil
juice of ½ lemon, or more to taste
½ tsp Dijon mustard
sea salt and black pepper

————

To make the mayonnaise, place the egg yolk in a clean bowl, with a damp tea towel underneath to keep it steady. With a balloon whisk, lightly whisk the yolk, then start to whisk in the oil a few drops at a time – this seems slow but we have had so many 'mayo splits' that it's worth taking your time. Adding a few drops of lemon juice as you go also makes it less likely to split. After each addition of oil, make sure it is all combined before adding the next, whisking continuously until the mixture becomes thick and 'mayo-like'. Continue until all the oil has been used. Add the lemon juice and mix. Add the mustard and salt and pepper to taste. Set aside.

Heat a dry frying pan until hot, add the fennel seeds and toast for a couple of minutes, stirring a few times, until fragrant and just starting to brown. Tip on to a plate and set aside to cool.

Peel the celeriac and shred into fine matchsticks. Add to a bowl and squeeze over the lemon juice. Add the mayonnaise, yoghurt, mustard, parsley and toasted fennel, and mix together. Season to taste and serve.

maple & honey roast
ham with watercress

1 unsmoked, boneless gammon
   joint, about 2.5kg
1 cinnamon stick
1 onion, peeled and halved
3 bay leaves
small handful of cloves

for the glaze and top
150ml maple syrup
100ml honey
1 tbsp English mustard
handful of cloves

for the watercress
3 bunches of watercress
olive oil, to taste
lemon juice, to taste
sea salt and black pepper

———

Put the gammon in a large pan filled with water, so the water is covering the whole of it (if not quite, then make sure you turn the gammon over halfway through cooking).

Add the cinnamon, onion, bay leaves and cloves to the pan and bring to the boil, then turn the heat down and simmer for around 1 ½ hours, skimming the surface every so often to remove the scum that rises. Remove the pan from the heat and strain off the liquid (you can save this for soups).

Preheat the oven to 200°C/gas 6 and put the ham in a foil-lined roasting tray to rest while you make the glaze.

Whisk the maple syrup, honey and mustard together to combine. If there is skin on the ham, remove and discard, then score the fat with a knife both ways to form a diamond pattern. Push a clove into the middle of each scored cross, covering the outside of the ham with cloves. Brush half of the glaze over the top, giving it an even coating.

Roast in the oven for around 10 minutes and then take out of the oven and brush over the remaining glaze. Put back in the oven for around 15–20 minutes, or until the top is golden brown. Watch it carefully to ensure the glaze doesn't burn. Rest the ham for at least 15 minutes before serving – meanwhile you can prepare the watercress.

Wash the watercress and add to a big serving bowl. Add olive oil, lemon juice and seasoning to taste, and toss lightly to mix.

chocolate & ginger cake with sherry buttercream

(will feed 6 greedy people, or 12)

75g cocoa powder, plus extra for
    dusting
180g pitted Medjool dates, soaked in
    hot water until cool, then drained
2 balls of stem ginger in syrup, plus
    2 tsp of the syrup
150ml runny honey
150g coconut oil, melted
2 tsp vanilla extract
225g ground almonds
60g dark chocolate (70% cocoa
    solids), melted and cooled
2 tsp ground ginger
2 tsp baking powder
5 large eggs, lightly beaten
4 tbsp milk
crystallised ginger, to decorate

for the sherry buttercream
150g unsalted butter, at room
    temperature
300g icing sugar, sifted
3–4 tbsp sherry
1 tbsp stem ginger syrup

———

Preheat the oven to 170°C/gas 3½.

Line a 23-cm springform cake tin with non-stick baking parchment and dust with cocoa powder.

Put the drained dates, stem ginger balls and syrup, honey, melted coconut oil and vanilla extract into a food processor and process for a couple of minutes until you have a very smooth, thick paste.

Add all the remaining ingredients, except the eggs and milk, and blitz again very quickly – for no more than 30 seconds, just long enough to make sure it's mixed. Add the eggs and blitz for another 30 seconds, then add the milk and blitz for 10 seconds.

Pour the batter into the prepared tin and level the surface, then place in the pre-heated oven on the middle shelf for 45 minutes, or until a skewer inserted in the middle comes out clean. Don't open the oven door before 35 minutes have passed.

Leave to cool in the tin. Once cool, use the spring release to ease the cake out and slide on to your serving plate.

For the buttercream, beat the butter to soften it, then gradually add the icing sugar until it is all incorporated. Add the sherry and the stem ginger syrup. If it gets a little loose, just add more icing sugar.

When the cake is completely cool, cover it with the buttercream and decorate with the crystallised ginger.

the forager's table

serves 6

crudités with wild garlic dip
deep-fried courgette flowers with
   ricotta, honey & mint
whole roasted mackerel with sorrel yoghurt
new potatoes with fennel pollen
pineapple weed granita

You would be forgiven for thinking that foraging in the city
means looking through the 'whoops' section in Asda. However,
through hosting our supper club and exploring the surrounding
areas, we have found that our urban neighbourhood is bursting
with gems: sweet pea flowers, nettles, cherry plums, blackberries,
elderflower, purslane, figs and sloes, to name a few favourites.
Throughout the seasons there are so many things to look out
for. Laura grows the courgette flowers for this menu on her patio
and we found the wild garlic near a disused railway. Pineapple
weed is a bit rarer – it likes growing on farms and in cracks in
brick buildings, it tastes like pineapple cubes from pick 'n' mix.
Once you know what it is, you will spy it everywhere.

N.B. Do seek advice from an experienced forager and ideally
take him or her with you before you pick anything.

crudités with wild garlic dip

1 x 400g tin chickpeas, drained (or preferably from a jar)
juice of 1 ½–2 lemons, to taste
1 tsp white wine vinegar
2 tbsp tahini
100ml extra virgin olive oil, plus extra to serve
big handful of wild garlic leaves (about 30g), washed, dried and finely
    chopped, or 3 confit garlic cloves (see below), finely chopped
fine sea salt
selection of colourful seasonal vegetables, such as radishes and
    asparagus or cauliflower florets and purple carrots, to serve

———

Put the chickpeas, lemon juice, vinegar, tahini and oil in a blender and process everything together. Scrape into a bowl and stir in the chopped wild garlic or confit garlic. Season to taste with a little salt.

Drizzle with oil and serve with the vegetables.

Confit garlic
Preheat the oven to 160°C/gas 3. Break apart a whole garlic bulb into separate cloves, leaving the skins on. Place in a small ovenproof dish and add enough olive oil to just cover them. Bake in the oven for 25–35 minutes, depending on the size of the cloves, until the cloves are soft and easily pierced with a skewer or cocktail stick. Remove from the oven and leave to cool. Transfer the cooled garlic and the oil to a sterilised, airtight container and store in the fridge, where it will keep for at least a couple of weeks.

deep-fried courgette flowers with ricotta, honey & mint

Makes 12

1 large egg
40g plain flour
100ml cold sparking water
12 courgette flowers
about 1 litre sunflower oil, for deep-frying

for the stuffing
250g ricotta
small handful of mint leaves, finely chopped
finely grated zest of 1 lemon
sea salt and black pepper

to serve
drizzle of floral runny honey
micro herbs or red amaranth (for a pop of colour)

First make the batter. In a bowl, whisk the egg and flour together, then add the sparkling water and whisk lightly to remove lumps – don't over-whisk so you lose the air bubbles, as you want the batter to be light.

For the stuffing, put the ricotta, mint and lemon zest in a bowl, with salt and pepper to taste, and mix until combined.

Gently open the courgette flowers and pinch out the stamen. Place a large tablespoon of the stuffing into each flower. Pinch and twist the petals lightly to seal the top – you want to make sure the stuffing is sealed in the flower so it doesn't leak out while cooking.

Pour the oil into a large, heavy-based pan; it needs to come at least halfway up the sides. Place over a high heat until it reaches 180°C – to test whether the oil is ready, drop a bit of the batter in: if it sizzles and bubbles to the top, it's ready.

Lightly coat the courgette and stuffed flowers in the batter and gently lower into the oil. Do this in batches so they don't stick together, and be careful when lowering them in as the hot oil will spit. Fry for about 2 minutes until light-golden brown and crispy. Using a slotted or wire spoon, transfer to kitchen paper to drain off the excess oil.

Serve immediately, with a drizzle of honey and a sprinkling of micro herbs and sea salt.

whole roasted mackerel with sorrel yoghurt

6 mackerel, gutted (ask your fishmonger to gut the fish for you if you prefer)
6 slices of lemon, cut into 12 half moons
12 bay leaves
olive oil, to drizzle
sea salt and black pepper

for the sorrel yoghurt
1 small garlic clove
small handful of sorrel leaves, roughly chopped
200g Greek yoghurt
3 tbsp olive oil
squeeze of lemon juice

―――――

Preheat the oven to 200°C/gas 6.

Season the fish on the inside and on both outer sides, and place in an ovenproof dish. Using a knife, make 2 incisions into the top of each fish, in diagonal parallel lines, then stuff a lemon half moon and a bay leaf into each incision. Drizzle with plenty of oil and roast in the oven for 20–25 minutes, until cooked through; the flesh should be white and opaque.

Meanwhile, make the sorrel yoghurt. Put the garlic, sorrel and a little salt into a pestle and mortar and crush to a green paste. In a bowl, mix the yoghurt, olive oil, lemon juice and some salt and pepper, then stir in the sorrel and garlic paste. Taste and adjust the seasoning and lemon juice to suit your palate.

Serve the fish on a lovely platter with the yoghurt alongside – tell your guests to check for bones!

new potatoes with fennel pollen

700g salad potatoes, such as Anya, Jersey Royals or small Yukon Gold, scrubbed
2 tbsp good-quality extra virgin olive oil
25g butter
1 tsp sea salt (try smoked sea salt)
½ tbsp ground black pepper
1 tbsp fennel pollen

―――――

Cook the potatoes in boiling, salted water for 12–15 minutes, or until just tender when prodded with a fork, then drain.

Crush the potatoes slightly with a fork, then stir in the oil, butter, salt and pepper. Scatter over the fennel pollen and stir again.

pineapple weed granita

1 litre water
400g granulated sugar
1 tbsp runny honey
70g pineapple weed (you want the flower heads and the leaves around the head,
    but discard everything else)
pared zest of 2 lemons and juice of 1

———

Heat the water, sugar and honey in a heavy-based pan over a low heat, until the
sugar has dissolved. Add the pineapple weed and lemon zest and raise the heat
to simmer for 5 minutes, making sure all the flower heads are submerged in the
sugar syrup. Remove from the heat, add the lemon juice and leave to infuse at
room temperature for at least 12 hours.

Line a colander with muslin or a clean tea towel and strain the liquid through
this into a saucepan. Discard any bits left in the muslin. Put the saucepan over
a high heat and bring to the boil, then turn down to a gentle simmer and let the
liquid reduce by a third (at this point you could transfer the liquid to sterilised
bottles and use as a cordial – it will keep in the fridge for 3 months).

Transfer the mixture to a shallow dish or plastic freezer container and freeze
until solid; depending on your freezer this could take anything between 1 and
4 hours. Remove and break up the crystals with a fork, then put back in the
freezer for a further 2 hours.

Remove from the freezer and fork it again so it forms large, flaky ice pieces.
Cover and keep frozen until needed (it can be made a few days in advance).

Serve the granita in individual glasses.

east end cucina

serves 6

peach & goat's curd panzanella
malfatti with pecorino & sage
chocolate & hazelnut biscotti

_____

We served malfatti, gnocchi's little sister, at one of our first
supper clubs and we couldn't believe how simple they were to
make. We felt like Italian mammas rolling them in the kitchen
together. Cooked spinach in the mixture works well, too, and
gives them a slightly looser texture than chard.

This twist on a panzanella makes use of the juicy peaches of
summer and grilling them brings out a wonderful caramelised
flavour. The only thing that could improve this menu is a chilled
glass of Prosecco.

peach & goat's curd panzanella

250g ricotta
270g open-textured bread,
    such as ciabatta
olive oil, for drizzling and brushing
4 ripe, juicy peaches (nectarines
    work well too)
600g broad beans in pods, or
    240g frozen if not in season
200g green beans
100g frisée lettuce
large bunch of mint (about 40g
    picked leaves), leaves roughly
    chopped
sea salt and black pepper

for the dressing
3 tbsp walnut oil
2 tbsp sherry vinegar

Line a sieve with muslin and set it over a bowl. Place the ricotta in the lined sieve and allow it to drain, without squeezing or pressing it, for at least 1 hour.

Preheat the oven to 180°C/gas 4. Heat a ridged griddle pan over a high heat.

Roughly tear the bread into large chunks. Drizzle each piece very lightly with olive oil and sprinkle with salt, then place in a single layer on a baking tray and bake in the oven for about 15 minutes, until lightly crisp.

Cut the peaches in half, remove the stones and then cut into slices (no more than 6 per half) and brush both sides of each slice with olive oil. Griddle the slices for about 2–3 minutes on each side, or until marked with griddle lines. Transfer to a plate.

Pod the broad beans, if using fresh. Add (fresh or frozen) to a small pan of boiling water, then take off the heat and leave for 3–4 minutes to loosen the bitter skins and make them easier to remove. Drain and slip the beans out of their skins. Cook the green beans in boiling, salted water for 5 minutes, or until *al dente*. Drain and set aside to cool.

Whisk together the walnut oil and vinegar for the dressing, seasoning to taste. In a large bowl, combine the toasted bread pieces, griddled peaches, broad beans, green beans, frisée and mint. Pour over the dressing. Break the strained ricotta into bits and add to the other ingredients, then use your hands to turn everything over. The ricotta will break up and coat the other elements. Transfer to a large platter and let everyone share. Eat immediately – don't let it sit around!

malfatti with pecorino & sage

330g ricotta
1kg Swiss chard, tough stems removed
2 large eggs
65g '00' flour, plus extra for dusting
265g pecorino, finely grated
$^1/_3$ nutmeg, freshly grated
sea salt and black pepper

to serve
100g salted butter
small bunch of sage, leaves picked
$^1/_2$ lemon

Line a sieve with muslin and set it over a bowl. Place the ricotta in the lined sieve and allow it to drain in the fridge overnight, without squeezing or pressing it.

In a couple of batches, cook the chard leaves in a pot of boiling, salted water until tender but still vibrant, for about 3–5 minutes. Plunge into a bowl of cold water and leave the cold tap running over them for a minute. Squeeze thoroughly to wring out as much liquid as possible, then chop and press with kitchen paper to get even more out. Transfer to a food processor and chop for about 30 seconds, then wring it out again to remove any remaining liquid – it needs to be very dry! – and set aside to cool.

In a mixing bowl, combine the chopped chard, strained ricotta, eggs, flour, half the pecorino, the nutmeg, and some salt and pepper to taste.

Dust a tray with flour, then dust your hands with flour and roll the dough into 36 oval or round malfatti. You want them very lightly coated in the flour.

Bring a pan of lightly salted water to the boil, add the malfatti in batches of around 8–10 and simmer for about 3 minutes – they will float to the surface when cooked. Drain and keep warm in a pan, reserving a little of the cooking water.

Melt the butter in a large sauté pan. Add the sage leaves and cook until the butter begins to brown lightly. Remove the leaves before they turn very brown. Mix in a few spoonfuls of the reserved pasta water, then add the malfatti to the butter sauce. Toss to coat, season with salt and pepper and add a squeeze of lemon to taste. Serve straight away with the sage leaves and remaining pecorino sprinkled over.

chocolate & hazelnut biscotti

butter, for greasing
55g blanched hazelnuts
175g plain flour, plus extra
   or dusting
50g cocoa powder
½ tsp baking powder
pinch of salt
100g caster sugar
50g dark chocolate (70%
   cocoa solids), roughly
   chopped
3 large eggs, beaten
milk, to glaze

to coat (optional)
75g dark chocolate (70%
   cocoa solids), roughly
   chopped
75g blanched hazelnuts,
   toasted (see method)

———

Preheat the oven to 160°C/gas 3 and lightly grease a baking sheet with butter.

Place the hazelnuts in a small roasting tin and pop them into the oven for 10–12 minutes, shaking the tin once or twice during cooking, until they are golden brown. Remove from the oven, tip onto a chopping board and, once cool enough to handle, roughly chop. (If you are planning to coat the biscotti then toast the hazelnuts for that at the same time and set aside.) Meanwhile, increase the oven temperature to 190°C/gas 5.

Sift the flour, cocoa powder, baking powder and salt into a large mixing bowl. Add the sugar, chopped hazelnuts and chocolate. Stir to combine. Make a well in the middle of the dry ingredients and slowly start to add the beaten eggs, little by little, stirring it in to combine. You are aiming for a firm, not too sticky or loose dough, so you probably won't need to add all the egg. Bring it all together into a ball with your hands.

Dust a work surface with a little flour and turn out the mixture. Roll into a long sausage shape, about 30cm long and 3–4cm diameter, then transfer to the greased baking sheet. Brush the top with a little milk to glaze and bake in the oven for 20–25 minutes until it starts to look biscuity and dried out.

Remove from the oven and reduce the oven temperature to 100°C/gas ¼. Carefully slice the biscotti at an angle into 1-cm slices. Place the slices on the baking sheet and return to the cooler oven for about 45 minutes. Remove from the oven, turn the biscotti over and bake for another 30–45 minutes, or until fully dried out. Look for any areas of biscuit that don't look dry and sandy, and if there are any, return to the oven for another 5 minutes or until fully dried. Remove from the oven and transfer to a wire rack to cool. You can store them in an airtight jar so they don't go soft, or just dust in cocoa or icing sugar and serve.

To coat them, melt the chocolate in a heatproof bowl set over a pan of simmering water, making sure the base of the bowl isn't touching the water. Remove the bowl from the pan. Finely chop the 75g toasted hazelnuts and spread out on a plate. Dip one end of each biscotti in the melted chocolate and for some or all of them, roll the coated end in the finely chopped hazelnuts for an extra crunch.

pull out
all the stops

serves 6

deep-fried olives stuffed with ricotta
roast chicken with tarragon mayo
blood orange & radicchio salad
squash, sage & freekeh
blackberry ice cream with ginger biscuits

———————

Sometimes all we want is a quick and gratifying dinner that
lets us spend most of our time with our feet up. But on other
occasions we love nothing more than spending all day cooking.
This is a menu for that kind of escapism. Admittedly, there
are more processes than a few of our other menus (please don't
be put off by deep-frying at home, for instance), but we promise
the end results are worth it. The ginger biscuit dough freezes
incredibly well, which is a great time-saver.

With this selection of dishes you'll want to set the mood
to match. Something sophisticated, paying attention to little
touches like place settings and playlists.

deep-fried olives with ricotta

50g ricotta
½ tsp finely grated lemon zest
150g green olives (we love Castelvetrano/Nocellara),
    pitted
100g panko breadcrumbs
50g plain flour
1 egg, beaten
sunflower oil, for deep-frying
sea salt and black pepper

———

Mix the ricotta and lemon zest together in a bowl and
season with salt and pepper. Dry the pitted olives with
kitchen paper and stuff each one with some of the
ricotta mixture, using a spoon or your fingers.

Put the breadcrumbs into a freezer bag and bash them
to a slightly finer crumb – this helps them stick better
to the olives. Set out 3 dishes and put the flour in
one, the beaten egg in another and the breadcrumbs
in the third. Dip each olive first in the flour, then the
egg, and finally coat in breadcrumbs. Set them aside.

Add sunflower oil to a heavy-based saucepan to come
to a depth of about 5cm. Set it over a high heat and
heat to 180°C. If not using a thermometer (although
it helps!), test it is ready by dropping in a large panko
breadcrumb – if it sizzles, the oil is ready to go.

Using a slotted spoon, carefully lower the olives into
the hot oil. Depending on how large your pan is, you
may be able to add them all at once – otherwise, fry
them in batches. When they are golden brown (this
will take about 40 seconds), take them out and place
on kitchen paper to drain off excess oil. Serve warm.

roast chicken & tarragon mayo

1 lemon, halved
3 garlic cloves
small handful of lemon thyme
1 medium chicken, about 1.5kg
sea salt and black pepper

for the tarragon mayo
170g Greek yoghurt
3 tbsp mayonnaise (see page 145 for home-made)
juice of ½ lemon
30g capers, well-rinsed
15g tarragon, leaves only, finely chopped
1 tbsp olive oil

———

Preheat the oven to 200°C/gas 6. Put the lemon
halves, garlic and thyme into the cavity of the
chicken and season the skin.

Put the chicken in an ovenproof dish and roast for
1 hour–1 hour 15 minutes, until the juices run clear.
(We like to turn up the temperature to 240°C/gas
9 for the last 5 minutes to make the skin extra-crispy.)
Remove the chicken from the oven and leave to rest
for 10–15 minutes.

Meanwhile, mix all the tarragon mayo ingredients
in a bowl, with salt and pepper to taste. For a
sharper sauce, add more lemon juice and balance
this with good-quality sea salt.

blood orange & radicchio salad

40g hazelnuts
4 blood oranges (use regular oranges
    or 2 grapefruits if not in season)
2 tbsp extra virgin olive oil
juice of ½ lemon, or to taste
1 tsp honey, or to taste
1 pink radicchio, washed and torn into big pieces
1 red chicory bulb, leaves separated
250g ricotta
sea salt and black pepper

———

Preheat your oven to 160°C/gas 3. Spread out the hazelnuts on a baking tray and toast in the oven for about 10–12 minutes, keeping an eye on them and shaking the tray a couple of times to move them around. When they start to turn golden brown and have a lovely, nutty aroma, remove and tip on to a plate.

Slice the very top and bottom off each orange so they have flat bases on which to sit. Using a sharp knife and working from top to bottom around the contours of each fruit, remove the peel, making sure you take off the pith as well.

Slice 2 of the oranges into rounds, and segment the other 2, running a sharp knife between the membranes to release the segments. Squeeze excess juice from the offcuts into a bowl.

For the dressing, add the olive oil, lemon juice and honey to the orange juice, along with some salt and pepper.

Put all the leaves in a large bowl and toss the dressing through them, adding more seasoning if necessary. Arrange the leaves on a large serving platter, layering them with dollops of ricotta, toasted hazelnuts, the orange slices and segments.

squash, sage & freekeh

about 1kg squash (any variety),
    cut into crescents 2cm thick
olive oil, for drizzling and dressing
handful of sage leaves
175g freekeh
300ml good-quality chicken stock
juice of ½ lemon
sea salt and black pepper

to serve
2 tbsp pomegranate molasses
30g pine nuts, lightly toasted in a dry frying pan
100g pomegranate seeds

———

Preheat the oven to 180°C/gas 4.

Place the pieces of squash flat on a baking try, drizzle with
lots of oil and sprinkle with salt and pepper. Roast in the oven
for 20 minutes until soft, scattering over the sage leaves for
the last 5 minutes of roasting, so that the sage leaves crisp up
and release their beautiful aroma.

Meanwhile, rinse the freekeh under cold, running water and
put in a pan. Add the stock, bring to the boil and boil over
a medium heat for 25 minutes, until tender. Drain and dress
with the lemon juice and some olive oil, seasoning to taste.
Transfer to a serving platter.

Arrange the roasted squash crescents and sage leaves over the
freekeh, then drizzle over the pomegranate molasses. Sprinkle
over the toasted pine nuts and pomegranate seeds, and serve.

blackberry ice cream with ginger biscuits

for the blackberry ice cream
4 large egg yolks
185g caster sugar
350ml whole milk
1 vanilla pod, split lengthways and seeds scraped out
600ml double cream
300g blackberries

———

First make the custard for the ice cream. Using a balloon whisk, mix the egg yolks and 125g of the sugar in a heatproof bowl. Put the milk, vanilla seeds and pod in a pan and heat until steaming, then pour in a slow stream on to the egg yolk mixture, whisking all the time. Rinse out the saucepan and transfer the mixture back to the pan. Place over a low-medium heat and stir gently with a wooden spoon; it will slowly start to thicken. Once the custard thickens to double cream consistency, strain through a sieve into a clean bowl. Add the cream, mix well and leave to cool for an hour.

Put the blackberries, the remaining 60g sugar and 30ml water in a pan over a medium heat. Leave to simmer for 10–15 minutes until the fruit has broken down, then strain through a sieve into a bowl. Leave to cool, then stir into the cooled custard.

Churn the mixture in an ice-cream machine for 40 minutes, following the manufacturer's instructions. Transfer to a loaf tin or freezerproof container and freeze for at least 2 hours. If you don't have an ice-cream machine, pour the mixture into a container and freeze overnight. The next day put it into the large bowl of a food processor and blitz until smooth. Scrape back into the container and re-freeze. Once solid, repeat the blitzing and then it should be good to go.

for the ginger biscuits (makes about 30)
100g unsalted butter, softened
80g caster sugar
1 tsp vanilla extract
1 tsp baking powder
½ tsp ground ginger
¼ tsp ground allspice
2 tbsp golden syrup
160g plain flour

———

Preheat the oven to 180°C/gas 4, and line a baking tray with baking parchment.

Cream the butter and sugar together until light and fluffy. Add the vanilla, baking powder, spices and syrup, and mix until well combined. Add the flour and bring it all together into a ball with your fingertips. Divide the dough in half and roll into 2 batons, about 2–3cm in diameter. Place the batons on the lined tray, leaving enough space between them as they will spread in the oven and you don't want them to stick together.

Bake in the oven for 15 minutes, until the biscuits have gone flat and golden brown in colour. Leave to cool for just 5 minutes then, while they are still hot, use a very sharp knife to cut the biscuits into 2-cm strips. Leave to cool and crisp up.

Serve the biscuits with a scoop of blackberry ice cream. Any left over can be stored in an airtight container for a couple of days.

d.i.y. thai

serves 6

summer rolls with dipping sauces
dom's thai green curry
mango & orange blossom swirl
    with sesame snaps

———————

We love Thai food: all those sweet, salty and sour flavours
combined. This is a meal that we've been fortunate enough to
have cooked for us by our friend Dom, who is a wizard at Thai
cooking. Luckily, he has shared his failsafe curry recipe with
us. The D.I.Y. element of this menu gets everyone involved
and, as there is a real knack to rolling, it can get enjoyably messy
too. It's lovely to make these home-made dipping sauces for
a more authentic taste, but if you're short on time you could
opt for shop-bought hoisin and chilli sauces.

summer rolls
with dipping sauces

6 carrots, cut into matchsticks (or julienned
    if you have a mandoline)
2 cucumbers, halved, seeds removed
    and sliced into half moons
300g radishes, finely sliced
300g bean sprouts
2 bunches of spring onions, sliced on
    the diagonal
3 avocados, halved, stoned, peeled
    and thinly sliced
bunch of coriander, thick stalks removed
bunch of mint, thick stalks removed
3 red chillies, finely sliced
1 packet of medium spring roll rice paper
    wrappers (about 3–4 per person)
cooked shredded chicken, prawns and/
    or tofu (optional)

for the chilli dipping sauce
2 tbsp toasted sesame oil
juice of 1 large lime
1 tbsp fish sauce
1 red chilli, finely sliced (seeds in or out
    according to how hot you like it)
1 tbsp runny honey
1 garlic clove, finely chopped

for the peanut dipping sauce
4 tbsp crunchy peanut butter
1 tbsp hoisin sauce
juice of 1 large lime
3 tbsp toasted sesame oil
1 ½ tbsp runny honey
1 ½ tbsp cider vinegar

For the chilli dipping sauce, add all the ingredients to a bowl and mix, then transfer to a small serving bowl.

For the peanut dipping sauce, whisk all the ingredients together in a bowl with 1 tablespoon of water, until you have the consistency you want (we like it thick enough to coat but thin enough to be able to dip), adding more water if you need to. Transfer to a small serving bowl.

Arrange all the vegetables, herbs and chillies on a large sharing platter. Serve in the middle of the table with the dipping sauces, a bowl of warm water and the rice papers alongside. Place the chicken, prawns and/or tofu, if using, in separate dishes.

Let each guest immerse a rice paper wrapper in the warm water for about 10 seconds, until the paper has become translucent and soft. Place the wet rice paper on a clean plate and load up with the vegetables, herbs and chilli, and the chicken, prawns and/ or tofu, if using. Roll up and tuck in the edges – this doesn't have to be neat! Dip immediately into the dipping sauces and enjoy.

dom's thai green curry

2 x 400ml tins coconut milk
500ml vegetable stock
3 star anise
4 kaffir lime leaves
40ml fish sauce
1 tbsp palm sugar
2 lemongrass stalks, bashed
1 sweet potato, peeled and cut into 3-cm chunks
1 aubergine, cut into 3-cm chunks
2 large Italian red peppers (the long ones),
    sliced into rings
1 courgette, sliced
200g cavolo nero, stems removed, leaves shredded
200g mangetout, halved
200g broccoli florets
360g basmati rice, to serve

for the curry paste
3 tbsp groundnut oil
2 medium banana shallots, roughly chopped
3 large garlic cloves, roughly chopped
2 green chillies, roughly chopped
grated zest of 2 limes
4–6-cm piece of fresh ginger, roughly chopped
25g fresh coriander
1 tsp toasted coriander seeds

to finish
Thai basil, coriander and mint leaves, chopped
finely chopped red chillies
lime juice
toasted coconut shavings

Put all the ingredients for the paste into a mini chopper or small food processor and process until smooth. Scrape the paste into a large frying or sauté pan and cook, stirring, over a medium heat for about 5 minutes, until aromatic and slightly darker.

Stir in the coconut milk, stock, star anise, lime leaves, fish sauce, sugar and lemongrass. Add the sweet potato and leave to cook for 10 minutes, then add the aubergine and cook for a further 10 minutes. Add the peppers and cook for 5 minutes, then add the rest of the vegetables and cook for another 5–7 minutes.

Meanwhile, cook the rice according to the packet instructions.

To finish, stir through the Thai basil, coriander, mint and chillies, sprinkle over lime juice to taste, and some toasted coconut. Serve with the rice.

mango & orange blossom swirl with sesame snaps

2 large, very ripe mangos
juice of 2 large limes
4 tbsp runny honey
1 tsp orange blossom water, or to taste
4 passion fruit
600g full-fat Greek yoghurt (ideally Total brand)
2 x 30g packets of sesame snaps, finely chopped

————

Peel and stone the mangos and put the flesh into a blender (we use a NutriBullet) with the lime juice and honey. Blitz until you have a purée. Stir in the orange blossom water and taste, adding more if you think it needs it. Halve the passion fruit, scoop the pulp out into the purée and stir to combine.

Put the yoghurt in a bowl and give it a little whisk to loosen it up. Fold in two-thirds of the mango purée mixture – you want the mango to be visible as a swirl, so don't over-fold.

Divide between six glasses or one large serving dish, and pour the remaining purée over the top. Refrigerate for 1 hour.

Serve with the chopped sesame snaps sprinkled over the top.

a reason to celebrate

serves 6

burrata with asparagus & nigella seeds
courgettes with mint & chilli
roast chicken, watercress & pistachio salad
lily's party cake
campari granita

———————

We made this menu for a friend's birthday, and we were besieged with requests for the recipes for every single element. No one can resist a plate of creamy burrata and certainly nobody has ever turned down a slice of our friend Lily Vanilli's cakes. Her East End bakery, just off Columbia Road flower market, is a constant source of inspiration and a regular pit stop, so we had to include one of her creations here.

burrata with asparagus & nigella seeds

2 bunches of asparagus
3 tbsp extra virgin olive oil, plus extra for brushing
juice of ½ lemon
3 burrata
1 tbsp nigella seeds
pinch of chilli flakes
sea salt and black pepper

———

Snap off the woody ends of the asparagus; they will each have a different natural breaking point.

Heat a griddle pan over a medium heat. Brush the asparagus spears with olive oil, sprinkle with salt and pepper and grill for 10–12 minutes (you may need to do this in batches), until they are lightly charred. Remove to a shallow bowl.

Whisk the 3 tablespoons of oil and the lemon juice together and use this to dress the asparagus. Transfer to a large serving platter, break up the burrata and scatter on top, then sprinkle over the nigella seeds and chilli flakes.

courgettes with mint & chilli

6 large courgettes
juice of ½ lemon
1 tbsp extra virgin olive oil
handful of mint leaves
pinch of chilli flakes
sea salt and black pepper

———

Using a speed peeler or mandoline, shave the courgettes into long, thin ribbons.

Put them into a bowl with a sprinkling of salt and leave to stand for 5 minutes to get rid of any excess water. Rinse well then pat dry with a clean tea towel or kitchen paper.

In a clean bowl, whisk together the lemon juice and olive oil, then add the courgette ribbons, lightly toss and season.

Transfer to a serving platter, tear over the mint leaves and sprinkle with the chilli flakes.

roast chicken, watercress & pistachio salad

1 medium chicken, about 1.5kg
1 lemon, halved
3 garlic cloves
small handful of lemon thyme
sea salt and black pepper

for the watercress and pistachio salad
½ baguette
4 tbsp olive oil
2–3 tbsp mayonnaise (for home-made
    see page 145)
5g lemon thyme, leaves picked
5g tarragon, leaves picked and roughly
    chopped
50g shelled pistachios
2 avocados
3 large ripe tomatoes, roughly chopped
    (or a handful of cherry tomatoes)
200g watercress, woody stalks removed
150g gorgonzola
1 radicchio head
2 chicory bulbs (ideally 1 red, 1 green)
juice of ½ lemon
extra virgin olive oil, to taste

Preheat the oven to 200°C/gas 6.

Stuff the chicken cavity with the lemon halves, garlic and thyme, then season the skin. Put into a roasting dish and roast for 1–1 ¼ hours, or until the juices run clear (you may need to adjust the cooking time if your chicken is a bit smaller or larger than 1.5kg). We like to turn the temperate up to 240°C/gas 9 for the last 5 minutes to make the skin extra crispy. Remove from the oven and leave to cool.

To make croûtons for the salad, tear your baguette into bite-sized pieces, place on a baking tray, drizzle with the olive oil, making sure it is well coated, and season with salt and pepper. Toast in the oven for 10 minutes, until lightly golden, then remove and set aside.

Once the chicken is cool, tear off all the meat into bite-sized pieces and place in a bowl. Add the mayonnaise, lemon thyme and tarragon, mix well, season and set aside.

In a small, dry frying pan, toast the pistachios over a medium heat until brown and fragrant. Remove from the pan and leave to cool, then roughly chop and set aside.

Halve and stone the avocados, scoop out the flesh, cut into chunks and place in a second large bowl. Add the tomatoes, watercress and chopped pistachios, then crumble in the gorgonzola. Tear up the radicchio and chicory leaves and add these to the bowl, along with the croûtons. Dress with the lemon juice and extra virgin olive oil. Season and lightly toss, then add the chicken mixture. Assemble on a large sharing platter.

lily's party cake

175g unsalted butter, softened, plus extra for greasing
330g plain flour, sifted
320g caster sugar
1 ½ tbsp baking powder
pinch of salt
3 eggs, at room temperature
190ml whole milk
1 ½ tsp good-quality vanilla extract

for the vanilla buttercream
100g unsalted butter, softened
300g icing sugar, sifted
1 tsp good-quality vanilla extract
75ml double cream

Preheat the oven to 200°C/gas 6. Grease and line two 23-cm cake tins.

In a bowl, or stand mixer, whisk together the dry ingredients. Using a hand-held electric whisk, or a stand mixer, beat in the butter until it is incorporated and the mixture looks like a fine crumble mix, for about 2–3 minutes on medium speed.

Add the eggs and beat, first on a medium speed, then on high, until just incorporated. Add the milk and vanilla extract and continue to beat, on a medium speed, then on high, for about 5 minutes, until the mixture is aerated, smooth and well beaten; it should look lighter in colour.

Divide between the prepared tins and smooth the mixture out to the edges, making sure the surface is even. Bake in the oven for 25–30 minutes, or until a toothpick inserted into the centre comes out clean and the cakes start to pull away from the sides of the tin. They will have taken on a deep golden colour. Remove from the oven and leave to cool in the tins for 10 minutes before turning out on to a wire rack to cool completely.

For the buttercream, in a stand mixer or using a hand-held electric whisk, beat the butter for 4–5 minutes on a high speed. Add the icing sugar, vanilla extract and cream and continue to beat on a low speed to bring it together. Increase the speed to high and beat for another 2–3 minutes, stopping to scrape down the sides of the bowl occasionally to ensure everything is mixed in well.

When the cakes are completely cool, sandwich some of the buttercream between the two layers, then either cover the entire cake with the remaining buttercream or just add another layer to the top of the cake. Decorate with any combination you like of fresh fruit and berries, toasted nuts, and fresh flowers (either edible or decorative).

campari granita

400ml pure, squeezed pink grapefruit juice
100g granulated sugar
80ml Campari
25ml lime juice (from about 1 lime)
Prosecco (optional), to serve

———————

In a small pan, gently heat the grapefruit juice and sugar together until the sugar has dissolved. Remove from the heat and leave to cool completely.

Stir the Campari and lime juice into the cooled juice and transfer it to a shallow dish. Place in the freezer until solid – depending on your freezer this could take anything between 1 and 4 hours – then remove and break up the crystals with a fork. Put back in the freezer for 2 hours.

After this, remove from the freezer and fork it again so it forms large, flaky ice pieces. Cover and keep frozen until needed (it can be made a few days in advance).

Serve the granita in individual glasses and top with a splash of Prosecco, if you like.

span'ish' tapas

serves 6

padrón peppers
roasted chickpea salad
beetroot, goat's cheese & mint dip
walnut labneh
thin crispy flatbreads
spiced olive & lemon chicken
chocolate mousse with pine nut brittle

————————

This is a great melting pot of influences, hence the 'ish'. It draws flavours from North Africa and the Middle East as well as Spain. There are plenty of elements for people to nibble at so you can relax at the table until the sun has well and truly gone down. If you wanted to have more of a tapas-style snack, the padrón peppers, beetroot dip and labneh would be great with the flatbreads and a delicious glass of red wine (or cava and pomegranate for a nice twist on fizz).

If you are strapped for time, prepare everything in advance and then just char the peppers before serving. The mousse makes a gorgeous sweet hit at the end of the meal. For a more informal look, serve it in a big dish in the middle and let everyone help themselves (you can even use the brittle as a spoon!).

padrón peppers

500g padrón peppers
olive oil
sea salt

———

Preheat an overhead grill
to very high. Toss the
peppers in enough oil to
coat them lightly, then
place them in a tray under
the grill.

Keep turning the peppers
as they start to blister and
blacken – it will take about
10–15 minutes.

Serve straight away, tossed
in salt.

roasted chickpea salad

1 x 400g tin chickpeas, drained and patted dry
2 tbsp olive oil
2 tbsp smoked paprika
1 small red onion, sliced
450g ripe tomatoes, halved or quartered
1 celery stick, finely chopped
1 red chilli (deseeded if you like a bit less spice),
    finely chopped
small bunch of coriander
150g feta, crumbled
sea salt and black pepper

———

Preheat the oven to 180°C/gas 4.

Put the chickpeas into a roasting tin and drizzle over the oil. Add the smoked paprika and mix well, seasoning with some salt and pepper. Roast for 15–20 minutes, until golden and toasted, then remove from the oven.

Put the remaining ingredients in a large bowl or serving platter, then spoon in the roasted chickpeas and stir gently. Serve with a drizzle of the oil from the roasting tin.

beetroot, goat's cheese & mint dip

70g hazelnuts
500g cooked beetroot (either roast your own
    or use shop-bought)
2 garlic cloves, crushed
50g Greek yoghurt
1 tbsp extra virgin olive oil, plus extra to serve
grated zest and juice of 1 lemon
40g firm goat's cheese log
handful of mint leaves
sea salt and black pepper

Preheat your oven to 160°C/gas 3. Spread half the
hazelnuts out on a baking tray and toast in the oven
for about 10–12 minutes, keeping an eye on them
and shaking the tray a couple of times to move them
around. When they start to turn golden brown
and have a lovely, nutty aroma, remove and tip on
to a chopping board. Leave to cool before roughly
chopping.

Transfer the nuts to a blender with the beetroot,
garlic, yoghurt, olive oil and lemon zest and juice.
Whizz to a smooth paste and season with salt and
pepper, adding more lemon juice to taste if you
think it needs it. Transfer to a small bowl.

Roughly chop the remaining hazelnuts and place
in a small bowl. Crumble the goat's cheese over
the top of the dip and sprinkle over some pepper
and the mint. Add a drizzle of olive oil and serve
with the chopped hazelnuts for sprinkling.

walnut labneh

500g natural yoghurt
40g walnut halves
extra virgin olive oil, for drizzling
sea salt and black pepper

———

Line a bowl with a piece of cheesecloth or muslin. Spoon the yoghurt into the muslin and gather the edges of the cloth up around it, tying a knot at the top. Hang the ball of yoghurt over the bowl (we usually tie it to a wooden spoon and wedge that in a cupboard door) for 4–6 hours. After about 4 hours, the dripping will have slowed right down and after 6 it should have stopped completely and the yoghurt will now resemble a soft goat's cheese, but may still be creamy in the middle.

Heat the oven to 160°C/gas 3. Spread the walnuts out on a baking tray and toast in the oven for about 10–12 minutes, keeping an eye on them. When they start to turn golden brown and have a lovely, nutty aroma, remove and tip on to a chopping board. Leave to cool before roughly chopping.

Lift the cheese out of the cloth, transfer to a plate and put in the fridge to lightly chill it.

To serve, spread the cheese out over a plate (like the way hummus is served in Lebanese restaurants). Season with salt and pepper, drizzle with olive oil and scatter the chopped walnuts on top. If you want a crunchy labneh, then just stir the nuts through it.

thin, crispy flatbreads

makes 12

400g strong white bread flour
30g unsalted butter, melted
pinch of sea salt

for the optional toppings
1 medium egg, beaten
dukkah, or a mixture of fennel and cumin seeds

———

In a large bowl, mix the flour with 120ml tepid water, the melted butter and salt, then form into a ball, adding more water if needed to bring it together. Knead the dough for 5 minutes until it is smooth and elastic, then wrap in cling film and let it rest for at least 1 hour (it can be left overnight).

Divide the dough into 12 balls and roll each one out to as thin as you can get it – around the thickness of a 20p coin. After resting, the dough might want to contract when you start rolling it, but persevere and it will eventually stay thin.

Heat a frying pan over a medium-high heat until very hot. Add a dough round and cook for 1–2 minutes until browning in patches on the underside. Flip and repeat on the other side, then remove to a wire rack while you cook the rest.

If adding a topping, brush egg wash over the top while the flatbread is still hot, then sprinkle over some dukkah or seeds. Serve warm or cool. They will keep in an airtight container for at least a week.

spiced olive & lemon chicken

6 chicken legs (thigh and drumstick), skin on,
    or 1.4kg chicken pieces of your choice
2 red onions, sliced
4 plum tomatoes, peeled and halved
3 garlic cloves, finely chopped
1 lemon, thinly sliced
100g pitted green olives
2 tsp paprika
2 tsp ground cumin
4 tbsp olive oil
225g cherry tomatoes, ideally on the vine
small bunch of flat-leaf parsley
sea salt and black pepper

———

Put all the ingredients, except the cherry tomatoes
and parsley, into a large bowl. Add 220ml water
and some salt and pepper, and mix together. Cover
and leave to marinate in the fridge for at least a few
hours, or overnight ready for the next day.

Preheat the oven to 200°C/gas 6.

Spread the chicken mixture out in a single layer in
a baking tray or dish, with the chicken skin side up,
and bake in the oven for 40 minutes. Add the cherry
tomatoes and continue cooking for another 20
minutes or until the chicken skin is coloured and
crisp, and the chicken is cooked through. Transfer
to a serving dish, if cooked in a baking tray, sprinkle
over the parsley and enjoy.

chocolate mousse
with pine nut brittle

300g dark chocolate
    (minimum 70% cocoa
    solids), broken into
    pieces
8 eggs, at room
    temperature
crème fraîche or
    mascarpone, to serve

For the brittle
50g pine nuts
75g caster sugar
flaky sea salt

———

First make the brittle. Preheat the oven to 180°C/gas 4. Spread the pine nuts out in a small baking tray and toast for 4–5 minutes, until they are just starting to brown – it's best to slightly under-toast them as they will continue to brown when you add them to the caramel. Keep a very close eye as they can quickly burn! Take out of the oven, tip on to a plate and leave to cool.

Place a piece of baking parchment over a flat, heatproof surface. Put the sugar and 2 tablespoons of water into a pan set over a medium heat. When the sugar has dissolved, increase the heat to medium-high and leave, without stirring (you can swirl the pan from time to time), until the mixture turns a caramel brown, keeping a careful eye on it. Stir in the toasted pine nuts, then pour the mixture on to the baking parchment and sprinkle with flaky salt. Leave to cool for at least 1 hour.

For the mousse, half-fill a pan with water, bring to the boil and then remove from the heat. Place the chocolate in a heatproof bowl and set the bowl over the pan, making sure the bowl does not touch the water. Allow the chocolate to melt, stirring occasionally to keep it moving.

Separate the eggs, placing 6 of the yolks in a jug and all 8 whites in a large, very clean bowl (keep the remaining 2 yolks for another use). Beat the yolks in the jug until combined, then slowly add them to the melted chocolate, whisking with a balloon whisk. The mixture will thicken instantly but keep whisking until you're sure it's smooth and well combined.

Whisk the whites until they form soft peaks. Using a large metal spoon, add a spoonful of whites to the chocolate mixture and beat well to combine. Add another spoonful and repeat until you can see the mixture start to slacken a little. Still using the metal spoon, gently fold in the rest of the egg whites, making sure the mixture is well combined (you don't want streaks of white in your mousse) but being careful not to over-stir, as you want to preserve as much of the air as possible to avoid a dense mousse. Either divide the mousse between individual serving glasses or add to one big bowl, and refrigerate for at least 3 hours.

Take the mousse out the fridge 15 minutes before serving. Break the brittle into shards and serve with the mousse, along with some crème fraîche or mascarpone.

eight 'til late

serves 6

cardamom & sage-infused gin & tonics
radishes with salt & butter
green peppercorn rack of lamb
roast cauliflower with almonds
roast aubergine with spiced garlic yoghurt
lemon drizzle with crème fraîche & pistachios

———————

Here we embrace the Middle Eastern flavours that we have
picked up on our travels (down the road to Ottolenghi's
restaurant). Having a rack of lamb is a real treat but we
understand it can end up being quite expensive for a lot
of people. If it feels like the pennies are totting up, try neck
of lamb instead.

Infusing gin to make a signature cocktail is so simple – have a
go with a variety of herbs and spices to create your own blend.
You can bottle any extra as take-home presents for guests,
to be enjoyed at a later date, or in the cab on the way home!

cardamom & sage-infused gin & tonics

radishes with butter & salt

10–15 sage leaves, plus extra to garnish
6–8 cardamom pods, crushed
1 x 700ml bottle of gin
3 x 1-litre bottles of tonic
chilled ice

1 bunch of radishes, ideally the elongated
French Breakfast variety, with leaves on
50g softened unsalted butter (we love Lescure,
a rich French butter)
1–2 tbsp good-quality flaky sea salt

———

———

Ideally, for a more intense infusion, start preparing this the morning of the dinner or even the evening before.

Push the sage leaves and cardamom into a swing-top bottle or similar and pour in the gin through a funnel. Put the lid on and leave to infuse in a dark place out of direct sunlight for 4 hours, or longer.

To serve, pour the gin over some ice in the glasses and top up with your required amount of tonic; we like to garnish each with a small sage leaf. If you aren't using all the gin and plan to store it for longer, strain into a clean bottle to remove the aromatics.

Cut each radish in half lengthways and place on a decorative serving board. Whip the butter until it becomes really soft and silky and add to the platter next to the radishes. Either sprinkle the salt on top of the butter or pile next to it.

green peppercorn rack of lamb

2 tbsp cumin seeds
2 tbsp green peppercorns (not in brine)
4 tbsp olive oil
3 racks of lamb, French-trimmed

———

Toast the cumin seeds in a dry frying pan until they become fragrant, then grind to a powder with the green peppercorns using a pestle and mortar. Add the olive oil to make a paste. Rub the paste all over the lamb, top and sides.

Put the pan back over a medium heat, add the lamb, skin side down, and sear for 5 minutes or so to help render the fat, then turn up the heat a little and sear the other side more quickly, as there is no fat to protect it. It should just be a light brown in colour.

Transfer the lamb to a roasting tin or baking tray and roast in the oven for 12 minutes for medium-rare or 15 minutes for medium. Remove from the oven and leave to rest – this is important, even if only for 5 minutes, although 10 minutes would be ideal. Carve and serve.

roast cauliflower with almonds

2 cauliflowers
4 tbsp olive oil
generous pinch of salt
squeeze of lemon juice
drizzle of pistachio or almond oil
20g mint, roughly chopped
30g flaked almonds, toasted

———

Preheat the oven to 190°C/gas 5.

Cut both cauliflowers into large slices and they should be easy to separate into medium florets. Cut away and discard any particularly chunky or hard core.

Spread out in a single layer on a baking tray (you may need two trays). Drizzle evenly with the olive oil, sprinkle over the salt and bake for about 45 minutes, giving the tray a shake every 5–10 minutes, until charred and crispy at the edges.

Tip into a wide serving dish and add a squeeze of lemon juice and a drizzle of pistachio oil. Sprinkle over the chopped mint and toasted flaked almonds. Serve warm or at room temperature.

roast aubergine with spiced garlic yoghurt

4 aubergines
4 tbsp olive oil
generous pinch of salt
30g pine nuts, toasted
10g fresh coriander, roughly chopped

for the spiced garlic yoghurt
6 tbsp Greek yoghurt
1 garlic clove, crushed
1 tsp harissa paste
1 tbsp sumac
½ tsp ground coriander

———

Preheat the oven to 190°C/gas 5. In a large bowl, mix all the yoghurt ingredients together and set aside until ready to serve.

Cut the aubergines in half lengthways, then slice across into half moons 2cm thick. Coat the slices in the oil, mix with the salt and spread out in a single layer in a baking tray. Roast in the oven for 25–30 minutes, until browned on the outside but still fleshy and pulpy.

Remove from the oven and allow to rest for a few minutes then, whilst still hot, drop the aubergine into the harissa yoghurt and turn to coat.

Serve warm or at room temperature, scattered with the pine nuts and coriander.

lemon drizzle with crème fraîche & pistachios

250g unsalted butter, softened,
    plus extra for greasing
250g caster sugar
50g poppy seeds
finely grated zest of 2 lemons
260g self-raising flour
50g ground almonds
5 medium eggs, beaten
140ml milk

for the icing and decorating
juice of 1 lemon
200g icing sugar, sifted
2 tsp poppy seeds (or edible flowers,
    if you have any)

to serve
400g crème fraîche
finely chopped pistachios

———

Preheat the oven to 180°C/gas 4. Butter a 900g loaf tin and line with baking parchment.

In a large mixing bowl, beat the butter and sugar together until light and fluffy. Add the poppy seeds and lemon zest, then beat in the flour and ground almonds.

In small jug, beat the eggs lightly with the milk then gradually add to the mixture, beating well, until thoroughly combined. Pour the cake batter into the lined tin and bake for 45–50 minutes, or until a skewer inserted into the centre comes out clean. Set aside to cool in the tin.

Meanwhile, make the icing. Add the lemon juice gradually to the sifted icing sugar to create a thick, smooth glaze, adding more juice to make it runnier or more icing sugar to make it thicker.

Once the cake has cooled, take it out of the tin and drizzle over the glaze, so that it falls down the sides of the cake. Scatter with the poppy seeds (or edible flowers). Slice the cake and serve on individual plates with crème fraîche and chopped pistachios or, if you're feeling lazy, serve on a big platter and let guests help themselves.

le weekend

serves 4

moules with d.i.y. garlic toasts
bavette, radicchio & anchovies
apple thin with crème fraîche

————————

When we are food shopping we are not usually roaming around
on a beautiful vintage bike with a baguette sticking out of the
basket; more likely we are crammed on the bus with too many
bags. But some of the pleasure of this menu is sourcing all
of the elements from local producers. So, to nail these dishes,
focus on great ingredients kept simple; it's what the French
do so well. We go to our local butcher for the steak, then pop
to the fishmonger for the mussels and the baker for some really
good-quality sourdough. All of the rest can be picked up at
the grocer.

moules

d.i.y. garlic toasts

1kg mussels
30g salted butter
3 banana shallots, finely chopped
4 garlic cloves, finely sliced
250ml white wine
juice of 1 lemon
250ml crème fraîche
small bunch of parsley, finely chopped
handful of samphire (optional – if in season)
sea salt and black pepper

———

Wash the mussels under cold running water. Throw away any with broken shells or that are open and don't close when you tap them lightly on the side of the worktop. Use a knife to scrape any barnacles off, and pull out any beards.

Melt the butter in a large, cast-iron pan, big enough to take all the mussels with the lid on. Add the shallots and garlic and sweat over a low-medium heat, until soft.

Add the mussels, wine and lemon juice, turn up the heat, then cover and steam the mussels open for 3–4 minutes, giving them a good stir every now and then.

Add the crème fraîche, parsley and samphire, if using, and remove from the heat.

Check for seasoning, adding a tiny pinch of salt if needed, and some black pepper. Serve in deep bowls with the garlic toasts.

4 whole garlic bulbs
30g butter, softened
1 sourdough loaf, sliced
flaky sea salt

———

Heat the oven to 200°C/gas 6.

Trim the top off each garlic bulb, making sure you keep the bulb whole. Place each bulb on a piece of foil. Push a teaspoon of the butter inside each, sprinkle with flaky salt, wrap the foil around each bulb and place on a baking sheet.

Bake for 45 minutes or until the garlic is very tender.

Griddle the sourdough slices until toasted on both sides, then let people squeeze the purée-like garlic out of their papery skins on to the sourdough. Spread with a knife, sprinkle with extra salt, and eat.

bavette, radicchio & anchovies

1kg bavette steak, cut into 3 equal pieces
olive oil
3 radicchios, cut into quarters
10–12 anchovy fillets in oil or marinated anchovies
    (the silver ones from a deli counter or jar)

for the salsa verde
2 garlic cloves, crushed
2 tbsp capers, well rinsed and roughly chopped
6 cornichons, roughly chopped
6 anchovy fillets in oil, finely chopped
65g parsley, tough stalks discarded, finely chopped
1 tbsp Dijon mustard
2 tbsp red wine vinegar
100ml extra virgin olive oil

———

For the salsa verde, put all the ingredients into a food processor and blitz until you have a sauce that is largely smooth but with a little texture.

Heat a griddle plan until really hot. Add the bavette, one piece at a time, and cook over a medium heat for 1 minute each side for rare, 2–2½ minutes for medium rare or about 3½ minutes for medium, giving the steak a 90 degree turn when you flip it, to create criss-cross griddle lines. Keep warm while you cook the remaining pieces.

While the bavette is cooking, rub olive oil over the radicchio quarters and add to the griddle, turning when each side colours.

Make sure all the steak pieces have rested for at least 5–10 minutes before slicing and arranging on a platter with the radicchios, adding anchovies here and there. Spoon the salsa verde over the steak and radicchios to serve.

apple thin
with crème fraîche

1 x 320g sheet of ready-rolled puff pastry
1 tbsp apricot jam
4 small dessert apples, cored, halved and finely sliced
1 tbsp melted salted butter
2 tsp soft light brown sugar
crème fraîche, to serve

Preheat the oven to 190°C/Gas 5.

Place the puff pastry sheet on a large piece of non-stick baking parchment and roll out until it is the size of a dinner plate.

Place a dinner plate on top of the pastry and trace around the plate with a knife, discarding the excess pastry. Transfer the pastry disc (still on the parchment) to a baking sheet. Use a very sharp knife to mark your inner border, by scoring a line 2cm inside the edge, cutting about halfway through the pastry.

Using a fork, prick a few holes across the surface of the pastry inside the border. Spread the apricot jam over the inner circle.

Arrange the apple slices in concentric rings over the jam, overlapping them tightly. Brush the apples lightly with the melted butter and sprinkle the sugar evenly over the whole tart.

Bake for around 35 minutes, until golden and cooked. Serve warm, with a dollop of crème fraîche.

movie night

serves 6

spiced nuts
sausage, broccoli & fennel seed pasta
salted caramel brownies

———————

These nuts last approximately four seconds; we've had to start rationing them when we make a batch. They are dangerously good matched with a glass of something cold and bubbly.

If you have a few friends coming over, this pasta is one step up from a takeaway pizza in the effort stakes and you'll get… well, brownie points… for the dessert.

spiced nuts

45g soft brown sugar
¼ tsp chilli powder
1 tbsp Chinese five spice powder
1 large egg white
1 tbsp light soy sauce
500g mixed nuts, such as Brazil nuts,
    almonds, pecans and cashews

———

Preheat the oven to 160°C/gas 3.

Mix together the sugar and spices.
Put the egg white in a large bowl.
Using a balloon whisk, whip the
egg white for a few seconds into a
foam. Stir in the soy sauce, followed
by the nuts. Turn them over to coat.
Sprinkle over the sugar and spice
mixture and mix everything
together well so that the nuts are
evenly coated.

Using a slotted spoon, transfer the
nuts to a lined baking sheet and
spread them out in a single layer.
Bake in the oven for 45 minutes,
turning them every 15 minutes
and separating any that have stuck
together.

Remove from the oven and leave to
cool. The nuts will become crisper
as they cool – some may stick
together, but you can just break
these apart with your hands.

sausage, broccoli & fennel pasta

1 ½ tbsp fennel seeds
200g Tenderstem broccoli
600g dried pasta (we like rigatoni and fiorelli)
1 tsp olive oil
9 sausages with a high pork content, skinned and each
    cut into 5 pieces
1 onion, finely diced
3 garlic cloves, finely chopped
1 red chilli, halved lengthways then cut across into slices
140ml white wine
juice of 1 lemon
sea salt
finely chopped flat-leaf parsley, to serve

———

Toast the fennel seeds in a dry frying pan set over a low heat,
until lightly browned. Tip onto a plate and set aside.

Cook the broccoli in boiling, salted water for 2–3 minutes
– so that it still has bite. Drain and rinse under cold water
to halt the cooking, then chop each stem in half lengthways.

Cook the pasta in boiling, salted water, according to the
timings on the packet, retaining a cup of the cooking liquor
before you drain. When the pasta has about 5 minutes to
go, add the oil to a large frying pan and fry the sausage pieces
over a medium heat, turning them to brown them all over.
Add the onion and turn the heat down to low. Add a good
pinch of salt and the garlic, and leave to soften for a minute
or two. Add the toasted fennel seeds, broccoli and chilli and
cook for another couple of minutes.

Add the wine and allow it to cook off. Toss in the drained
pasta, the lemon juice and a splash of the reserved cooking
liquor to loosen. Sprinkle with parsley to serve.

salted caramel brownies

100g dark chocolate (70% cocoa solids),
   roughly chopped
125g unsalted butter, plus extra for greasing
250g granulated sugar
2 large eggs
1 tsp vanilla extract
1 tsp flaky sea salt (smoked salt adds a great
   extra dimension)
100g plain flour
12 squares of milk chocolate containing
   caramel pieces (Cadbury's Caramel
   or Galaxy Caramel work for us)

———

Heat your oven to 170°C/gas 3. Line a baking
tin, 28 x 20cm, with baking parchment, leaving
extra up around the sides. (For nine deep
brownies use a 20 x 20cm square tin.)

Place the dark chocolate and butter in a large
bowl set over a pan of simmering water (make
sure the bottom of the bowl isn't touching the
water) and leave until just melted.

Take off the heat and use a balloon whisk to
whisk in the sugar, then the eggs, one at a time,
then the vanilla and half the salt. Gradually
sift in the flour then stir in using the whisk.

Pour the mixture into the tin, spreading it
out so that it is even. Press a piece of caramel
chocolate into the surface at regular intervals
(so that when cut into 12 there is a piece at the
centre of each, 9 if using a square tin) and
sprinkle the surface with the remaining salt.

Bake in the oven for 20–25 minutes, or until
a skewer inserted in an area with no caramel
comes out without raw batter on it. The
brownies should also be starting to come away
from the edges and gently cracking on top.
Leave to cool – or eat them when they're
straight out of the oven if you can't wait (and
while the centres are still runny).

curry night

serves 6

kale chana with burnt garlic
chapatis
green beans with mustard seeds
cardamom & rose water lassi

This is quicker to make than picking up the phone and ordering
from your local curry house; perfect for the sofa with a film and
a bottle of Tiger beer in hand. The chana is an adaptation that
has been round the houses and eventually fell into our hands
a few years ago – now we couldn't get through winter without it.

kale chana with burnt garlic

3 heaped tsp cumin seeds
1 tbsp coconut oil
2 large onions, finely chopped
4 garlic cloves, finely chopped
2 leeks, finely chopped
5-cm piece of ginger, grated
2 tsp ground coriander
2 tsp ground turmeric
1 tsp dried chilli flakes
2 x 400g tins coconut milk
400ml vegetable stock
3 tomatoes, chopped
2 x 400g tins chickpeas, drained and rinsed
3 tbsp mango chutney
250g kale, stalks removed, chopped
250g spinach, rinsed

for the burnt garlic
1 whole garlic bulb
1 tbsp olive oil

to serve
360g basmati rice
Greek or other thick yoghurt

Heat the cumin seeds in a large, dry pan over a medium heat, until they start to crackle, then add the coconut oil, onions, garlic and leeks. When soft, add the ginger, coriander, turmeric and chilli flakes, and increase the heat to cook for 2 minutes.

Add the coconut milk, stock, tomatoes, chickpeas and mango chutney. Stir well, then add the kale and spinach a little at a time, letting the leaves reduce down between additions. Cover with a lid, reduce the heat and simmer for 15 minutes.

Meanwhile, cook the rice according to the packet instructions, and make the 'burnt' garlic.

Separate out the garlic cloves, peel and finely slice them. Add, with the oil, to a pan over a medium heat and cook for about 5 minutes, stirring occasionally; you want the garlic to go a deep brown. Remove from the heat and set aside.

Take the chana off the heat. Serve with the rice and a bowl of yoghurt with the burnt garlic sprinkled on top.

chapatis

350g wholemeal flour, plus extra for dusting
170ml lukewarm water

———

Add the flour to a bowl and slowly add the water, stirring as you combine them and mixing with your hands to form a dough. Knead the dough on a floured work surface for 5 minutes until smooth and becoming elastic. Cover with a tea towel for 30 minutes to rest.

Divide the dough into 12 pieces and use a rolling pin to roll them out flat into little rounds, as thin as you can make them without tearing them.

Heat a dry frying pan over a medium heat until really hot, then cook the chapatis one at a time on each side as quickly as possible, until air bubbles appear and they start to blister. Remove to a plate and cover with a clean tea towel while you cook the rest. Serve as soon as all 12 are cooked.

green beans with mustard seeds

550g green beans, trimmed
2 tbsp groundnut oil
1 tsp cumin seeds
1 tbsp black mustard seeds
5 garlic cloves, peeled

———

Boil the beans in a pan of boiling water over a medium heat for 4–6 minutes, until tender but still retaining some bite.

Meanwhile, heat the oil in a frying pan and, when hot, add the cumin seeds and mustard seeds. When the mustard seeds start popping, crush the garlic cloves into the pan and turn down to a medium heat.

Use a slotted spoon to drain the beans and transfer to the frying pan. Stir to coat the beans in the oil and spices, cooking for a further 2 minutes. Remove from the heat and serve.

cardamom
& rose water
lassi

75g caster sugar
6 green cardamom pods, split open
2 tsp rose water
500ml plain yoghurt
about 150ml whole milk (more or less if you
    prefer thin or thick)
3 tbsp granulated sugar
handful of ice cubes
handful of unsalted pistachios, cut into slivers,
    to serve

———

For the syrup, put 100ml water in a pan
and add the caster sugar, cardamom pods
and rose water. Place on a medium heat until
the sugar has dissolved and the water has
evaporated enough to turn into a thick syrup.

Strain through a sieve and transfer to a
blender with the yoghurt, milk, granulated
sugar and ice cubes. Blitz until chilled,
smooth and frothy. Serve topped with the
slivered pistachios.

summer garden party

serves 12

grapefruit & amaro tonic
rocket fuel cocktail
watermelon with almond & dill
potato salad
rainbow tomatoes
roast salmon stuffed with watercress
elderflower pressé jelly
summer berry & pistachio pavlova

———————

For a while there, 'buffet' was a bit of a dirty word. But in the last 12 months we've been to more of them than sit-down dinners. Buffets are cool again – just ditch the vol-au-vents and turkey curry and keep it simple. Everything on this menu can be prepared in advance. Make your cocktails, stuff the salmon, cook your potatoes, bake the meringues, and have the jelly ready to go. Then all you need to do is slice some ripe tomatoes when people arrive and pop some ice in the drinks.

Hang strings of festoon lights above long trestle tables for the ultimate, picture-perfect party. The rocket fuel is our secret weapon – it gets people chatting without fail, and then chatting more until 2 a.m. when we have to kick them out.

grapefruit & amaro tonic

2 parts pink grapefruit juice
1 part vodka
1 part Stellacello or campari
1 part tonic water

to serve
ice
a slice of grapefruit

———

For both this and the rocket fuel cocktail (right), make up the cocktail in a jug so that it's easy to serve out to large numbers and so that people can refill their glasses when they're ready.

Fill each jug to about three quarters full with as many ratios of the main cocktail ingredients as will fit. When you're ready to serve, top the jugs up with ice and add the garnish. Get pouring promptly so that the ice doesn't melt and dilute the drinks.

rocket fuel cocktail

1 part gin
1 part elderflower cordial
2 parts Prosecco

to serve
ice
mint
cucumber

———

watermelon with almonds & dill

2 large banana shallots, thinly sliced into rounds
cider vinegar, for soaking
300g almonds, roughly chopped
1 small watermelon, peeled and cut into 2.5-cm cubes
300g feta
300g radishes, thinly sliced (ideally with a mandoline)
large bunch of dill (about 75g), roughly chopped
sea salt and black pepper

––––––––

Place the shallots in a bowl and pour over enough cider vinegar to cover. Mix, making sure all the shallots are coated in the vinegar, and set aside.

Place the chopped almonds in a dry frying pan over a low to medium heat. Toss until toasted and the skin has turned golden brown; this will only take about 5 minutes, so don't leave them unsupervised. Tip onto a plate to cool.

Place the watermelon in a large bowl and crumble over the feta. Remove the shallots from the vinegar and add them to the bowl, along with the radishes and toasted almonds. Scatter over the dill, season and mix well with your hands. Transfer to a large platter and serve.

potato salad

1.5kg mini new potatoes (the smaller the
    better), halved
1 tsp Dijon mustard
1 tbsp good-quality extra virgin olive oil
1 tbsp capers, well rinsed
roughly chopped herbs, such as dill,
    basil or parsley (optional)
sea salt and black pepper

———

Cook the potatoes in boiling, salted water
until cooked through, then drain and
set aside for a few minutes to cool down
a little. In your serving bowl, mix together
the remaining ingredients, except the
seasoning.

Add the drained, warm potatoes and turn
to coat thoroughly. Add salt and pepper
to taste, and serve.

rainbow tomatoes

1.2kg ripe tomatoes (a variety of different
    shapes and colours)
100g basil sprigs (purple and green for extra
    colour), leaves picked
60ml extra virgin olive oil
sea salt and black pepper

———

Roughly slice and chop your tomatoes – some
into halves, some quarters and some sliced.
You want a variety of textures, shapes and
sizes in the bowl; this doesn't have to be neat.

Place the tomatoes in a bowl and season with
salt and pepper. Tear over the basil leaves,
reserving a few to garnish. Add the olive
oil and lightly toss with your hands. Arrange
on a serving platter and top with the reserved
basil leaves.

roast
salmon stuffed
with watercress

115g unsalted butter, softened
grated zest and juice of 1 lemon
200g watercress, woody stalks removed,
    roughly chopped
120g breadcrumbs
1 small banana shallot, finely chopped
1 whole salmon, about 2–2.25kg, gutted
1 lemon, thinly sliced
sea salt and black pepper

———

Preheat the oven to 170°C/gas 3.

Put 90g of the butter, the lemon zest and half
the juice, the watercress, breadcrumbs, shallot
and plenty of seasoning in a bowl and mash
together with your hands until well mixed. Spread
the stuffing inside the cavity of the salmon.

Tie the salmon together at intervals with kitchen
string, so that the space between each set of ties is
roughly one portion – try to achieve equal portions
while taking into account that the salmon tapers
towards the tail end. Cut a slit in each segment of
salmon and insert a half-slice of lemon (you may not
need all the slices). You can protect the head and
thinner tail end of the fish with a layer of well-
greased foil, to slow their cooking.

Squeeze the remaining lemon juice over the fish
and spread the remaining 25g butter over the top.
Cook in the oven for 30 minutes, or until it is cooked
through but still pink, and is lovely and moist.

elderflower pressé jelly

1.2 litres elderflower pressé (sparkling elderflower)
80ml lemon juice (from 2 large lemons)
14 gelatine leaves
200ml elderflower cordial
20g edible flowers
200g raspberries
1 large ripe plum, sliced
1 large ripe nectarine, sliced
pouring cream, to serve

Put the elderflower pressé and lemon juice in a large bowl. Soak the gelatine leaves in a small bowl of cold water until soft, for about 5 minutes. Put the cordial into a small saucepan, warm through over a low heat, then remove from the heat.

Drain the gelatine and squeeze out excess water, then add to the warm cordial, stirring until it has dissolved. Add this mixture to the pressé and lemon juice and stir until evenly distributed. Put in the fridge for 30 minutes, then take it out and give it a stir. Repeat this 3 more times.

Take a 1.5 litre jelly mould or bowl. Ladle in enough of the jelly mixture to cover the base (this will be the top of the jelly). Choose some of your best flowers and fruit, place over the jelly and put in the fridge until set. At this stage, the remaining jelly will be almost like wallpaper paste, still pourable but capable of suspending fruit and flowers where they are placed. Add a little more jelly mixture on top of the set jelly, then a handful of flowers and fruit, refrigerate and repeat until you have used all the fruit and flowers (reserving some for decoration), finishing with a jelly layer to create a smooth base. Return to the fridge to set overnight.

When you are ready to serve, wet a serving plate so you can slide the jelly into position if you need to once it's tipped out. Fill your sink with warm water and submerge the bowl up to just below the top of the jelly for 30 seconds to loosen the sides. Using your fingers, gently pull the sides of the jelly away from the bowl, place your plate on top, flip over, give it a gentle shake and you should hear it drop. Lift off the bowl, decorate with flowers and berries, and serve with cream.

summer berry & pistachio pavlova

for the pistachio meringues
10 large egg whites
large pinch of salt
500g caster sugar (white is better than golden
  here)
140g shelled pistachios, chopped

for the topping
650ml whipping cream
25ml elderflower cordial (optional)
600g mixture of fresh fruit (strawberries, raspberries,
  blueberries)
45g shelled pistachios, roughly chopped
fresh mint leaves
fresh edible flowers (optional)

Heat the oven to 110°C/gas ¼. Line four baking sheets with baking parchment (you may need to cook the meringue in batches if you don't have enough baking sheets or oven shelves) and draw a circle 20cm in diameter on each sheet. Turn the sheets over so that the circles are visible from underneath.

Place the egg whites and salt in a large, clean bowl. Using an electric whisk, and starting on a low speed, whisk into a foam, then increase the speed a little and whisk until the whites stand in stiff peaks. Up the speed again and add the sugar a tablespoon at a time, whisking for about 5 seconds between additions, until all the sugar is incorporated and you have a glossy mixture. Now use a metal spoon to fold in the chopped pistachios.

Place a tiny dot of meringue underneath each corner of the sheets of parchment to hold them in place. Divide the mixture evenly between the four trays and, using the back of a large serving spoon, spread the mixture out to fill the four marked circles. Bake in the oven for 2 hours, then turn the oven off but leave the meringues in the oven until they are completely cold.

(At this stage, you can store the meringues in an airtight container, separating the discs with baking parchment; they will keep for a few days. Or you can freeze and use within 1 month.)

When ready to serve, whip the cream to soft peak stage, then stir through the elderflower cordial, if using. Spread the cream over the meringue discs and top with the fruit. Sprinkle over the chopped pistachios, mint leaves, and edible flowers, if you have some.

canapés for a crowd

serves 12

pea & mint crostini
crab in little gem
goat's cheese, honey & thyme dates
parma ham with celeriac rémoulade
chicory, roquefort & hazelnuts
smoked salmon & horseradish on rye
white bean dip
hazelnut & sea salt fridge fudge

———————

There is always an excuse for canapés – don't just reserve them for the big occasions. If you don't want to cook a full meal, a few of these snacks will keep a baying crowd happy. The secret with all of these is they are no-cook, all-assembly; perfect for the time-poor. No one wants a canapé that requires both hands – these are all designed to be eaten in one bite, so that everyone can keep hold of their tipple of choice. Serve on mismatched patterned platters and boards.

pea & mint crostini

makes 18–20

½ baguette
40–50ml olive oil, plus 2 tbsp for brushing
250g frozen peas
grated zest of 1 ½ –2 lemons, plus a squeeze of juice
50g feta, plus extra to garnish
small handful of mint leaves
sea salt and black pepper

———

Preheat the oven to 180°C/gas 4.

Cut the baguette into slices 5mm thick. Lay all the slices on a baking tray, brush with the 2 tablespoons of olive oil and season on both sides. Bake in the oven for 8–12 minutes until slightly golden and crisp – watch them carefully as they can quickly burn. Remove from the oven and set aside.

Put the peas in a heatproof bowl and cover in boiling water. Leave for 2 minutes then drain and add to a blender along with the lemon zest and juice, feta, olive oil (start with 40ml and add more to taste), mint (reserving 18–20 small leaves to garnish), and some seasoning. Blitz for a couple of seconds; we like our pea mixture to be rough, but if you like a smooth consistency, blitz for longer. Taste and check the seasoning – if you like it more zingy, add some more lemon juice.

Top the crostini with the pea mixture and arrange on a serving platter. Sprinkle each with a crumble of feta and a mint leaf.

crab in little gem

makes 24

400g crab meat (50/50 white and brown
    meat)
3 tsp mayonnaise (home-made is nicer,
    see page 145, but shop-bought is fine)
finely grated zest of 1 lemon and 1–2 tsp juice
pinch of dried chilli flakes
4 Little Gem lettuces
sea salt and black pepper
chopped chives, to garnish

————

In a bowl, mix the crab meat, mayonnaise,
lemon zest and juice, chilli flakes and
some salt and pepper – taste and check
for seasoning.

Prepare the lettuces: discard the large outer
leaves, separate out the smaller leaves, wash
and carefully dry, and place on a large serving
dish. Load up with the crab mix, then sprinkle
with the chives to garnish.

goat's cheese, honey & thyme dates

makes 12

100g soft goat's cheese
10 thyme sprigs, leaves only, plus a few extra
    to garnish
1 tbsp runny honey, plus extra to drizzle
12 Medjool dates, stoned

————

Put the goat's cheese in a bowl, add the
thyme leaves and honey and stir them
through the cheese.

Make an incision down the side of each date
to create an opening, but don't cut all the
way through. Fill each date with a spoonful
of thyme-flecked goat's cheese.

Serve immediately, with a sprinkling of
thyme leaves and a drizzle of honey, or store
in the fridge until later.

parma ham with celeriac rémoulade

makes 24

12 slices of Parma ham, each sliced in half

for the celeriac rémoulade with fennel seeds
2 tbsp fennel seeds
1 medium celeriac
juice of 1 lemon, or more to taste
5 tbsp mayonnaise (home-made is nicer,
    see page 145, or use shop-bought)
2 tbsp Greek yoghurt
4 tbsp Dijon mustard
large bunch of flat-leaf parsley, chopped
sea salt and black pepper

———

Heat a dry frying pan until hot and toast the fennel seeds for a couple of minutes, stirring a few times, until fragrant and just starting to brown. Remove, tip onto a plate and set aside.

Peel the celeriac and shred into fine strips, about a matchstick in thickness. Add to a bowl and squeeze over the lemon juice. Add the mayonnaise, yoghurt, mustard, parsley and toasted fennel seeds and mix together. Have a taste and check for seasoning, adding salt to taste. If you like it with more bite, add some more lemon juice.

Put a teaspoon or so of rémoulade on to each strip of Parma ham. Crack some black pepper over and roll up.

chicory, roquefort & hazelnuts

makes around 30

200g Roquefort cheese
75ml double cream
4 heads of chicory
3 tbsp finely chopped hazelnuts
truffle oil (optional)

———

Crumble the cheese into a food processer, add the cream and blitz until smooth. Transfer to a bowl.

Wash and dry the chicory, removing the outer larger leaves that are too big for mouth-sized pieces. Trim the base of the leaves you are using and arrange on a platter.

Fill each of the chicory leaves with some of the cheese mixture, about a teaspoon per leaf, sprinkle the nuts over the cheese and add a little drop of truffle oil, if using, on top of the nuts.

smoked salmon & horseradish on rye

white bean dip

makes 18–36 (depending on size)

3–4 slices of rye or pumpernickel bread
3–4 tbsp creamed horseradish
250g smoked salmon, cut into strips
10g dill sprigs
½ lemon
black pepper

———

Toast the bread and cut into 6 or 9 squares, depending on your preferred size of canapé. Dollop a small amount of the creamed horseradish on each as a base.

Place a strip of salmon on top (we usually roll ours first), top with a dill sprig and add a grind of black pepper. Squeeze lemon juice over the whole platter before serving.

3 x 400g tins cannellini beans, drained and rinsed
3 garlic cloves, crushed
juice of ½ large lemon, or more to taste
5 tbsp extra virgin olive oil, plus extra for drizzling
sea salt and black pepper

to serve
hot paprika (optional)
crisps, flatbreads or tortilla chips

———

Place the beans in a food processor and start to blitz. Add the garlic, lemon juice, olive oil and some salt and pepper and blend for 2 minutes – longer if you want a smoother consistency. Taste for seasoning and zingyness, adding more lemon juice if you think it needs it.

Scrape into a serving bowl and drizzle with olive oil. Sprinkle with hot paprika, if you like, and serve with crisps, flat breads or tortilla chips.

hazelnut & sea salt fridge fudge

100g hazelnuts
275g Nutella or chocolate spread
150g dark chocolate (60% cocoa solids),
    broken into pieces
1 x 400g tin condensed milk
flaky sea salt (optional)

———

Preheat your oven to 160°C/gas 3. Spread the hazelnuts out on a baking tray and toast in the oven for about 10–12 minutes, keeping an eye on them and shaking the tray a couple of times to move them around. When they start to turn golden brown and have a lovely, nutty aroma, remove and tip onto a chopping board. Leave to cool before roughly chopping. Set aside 20g for decoration.

Line a baking tin, 20cm square, with greaseproof paper.

Put the Nutella, dark chocolate and condensed milk in a heatproof bowl set over a pan of gently simmering water on a low heat (make sure the bottom of the bowl isn't touching the water) , and slowly melt. Remove from the heat then add the nuts (except the ones reserved for decoration) and stir thoroughly.

Pour into the lined tin, ensuring there is an even spread of nuts. Sprinkle the reserved extra nuts on top and sprinkle some salt over, if desired.

Cover and set aside to cool. Once cool, refrigerate for at least 2 hours, then turn out of the tin and cut into little squares to serve.

index

acknowledgements

There are so many people who have made these pages what they are. Thank you doesn't feel like enough. But here goes...

Quadrille – you have been our wonderful partners in this project. We remember washing up after our first supper club, wondering what we would do next (and whether we would even attempt a second!). You believed in us and helped to create a book we are so proud of. Sarah Lavelle and Helen Lewis, it's been our pleasure to work with people with such incredible vision, who take such care in what they do. You've taught us so much.

Kristin Perers – where do we begin? We love your spirit, your style, and… your homes! You really have taken extraordinary photographs and brought this book to life. We are so thrilled to now call you our friend too.

Sam – the greatest photography assistant ever (also especially good at hand-holding and making light work of leftovers).

Tabitha – your styling on this book far surpassed anything we could have ever have hoped for. An amazing eye and more amazing Zumba moves.

Aya – you are magic. Your food looked too good to eat, but eat it we did! We ate like kings, didn't we? Along with wonderful Charlotte, so much of the beauty of this book is down to you.

Kat – you made sure we meant a teaspoon not a tablespoon (and you were always right!). Incredible attention to detail, always innovative ideas.

Imogen – what a lifesaver you've been. Sometimes we thought we couldn't do this, and you were there with reassurance and a solution to every problem. Thanks for being our always reliable second opinion.

Katy and Terri aka WORM, we absolutely love you two. Your floristry is forward-thinking, your work ethic astounding and your talent enviable. The better-looking J&L.

Linda – you transformed the Haggerston patio into a Spanish oasis, and Rosie B, you made summer bloom in Clapton; we were so lucky to have you both on board.

Rachel Bakewell and Anna Cash – you made us look presentable for the cover. Well done and thanks.

Megan Riera – we were blown away by your beautiful calligraphy.

Hato Press – Ken, Cat and Ben – for many teas from the cafetière and so much more, thank you.

Helen Gleave at Insanity (second Mum) and Sophie and Jack at James Grant, the best in the biz. So much appreciation.

Alex and Nathan at Public Eye, Jordan, Naomi and Liz at LMPR and of course Rory Scarfe at Furniss Lawton – we love you all for caring so much and wanting the best for us and this book.

To those who appear in these pages in the form of their much-loved and much-used recipes; Lily Vanilli for your foolproof cake recipe, Dom for letting us 'borrow' your Thai curry recipe, and Ed for great flavour combinations including the favourite sausage pasta, thank you.

A lot of love to our friends for being taste-testers and supporting on shoot days; Jaime, James, Beckie, Laura A, Russell, Kitty, Elliott and Jamie W, Ben (for painting too) and Hannah and Rory. And to our super siblings Anna and Max for pretending it was always a pleasure and never a chore.

Jordan Bourke, Georgie Hayden and Rosie Birkett – your advice has been invaluable.

Jon Gorrigan – one of the most kind-hearted, generous, wonderful people we have ever met. J&L wouldn't be what it is without you. And yes we want you to cook us kale chana for the rest of our lives. Love you, JG.

Eileen – you are always at the other end of the phone with oven times, vegetarian alternatives and allotment knowledge. The best cooking is always in your kitchen, the best food at your table. Thank you for everything.

And finally, from J to L and L to J. I wouldn't want to be on this journey with anyone else.